THE HARMONY PROJECT WITH P3.EXPRESS

Other publications by Van Haren Publishing

Van Haren Publishing (VHP) specializes in titles on Best Practices, methods and standards within four domains:
- IT and IT Management
- Architecture (Enterprise and IT)
- Business Management and
- Project Management

Van Haren Publishing is also publishing on behalf of leading organizations and companies: BRMI, CA, Centre Henri Tudor, CATS CM, Gaming Works, IACCM, IAOP, IFDC, Innovation Value Institute, IPMA-NL, ITSqc, NAF, KNVI, PMI-NL, PON, The Open Group, The SOX Institute.

Topics are (per domain):

IT and IT Management	Enterprise Architecture	Business Management
ABC of ICT	ArchiMate®	BABOK® Guide
ASL®	GEA®	BiSL® and BiSL® Next
CMMI®	Novius Architectuur Methode	BRMBOK™
COBIT®		BTF
e-CF	TOGAF®	CATS CM®
ISM		DID®
ISO/IEC 20000	**Project Management**	EFQM
ISO/IEC 27001/27002	A4-Projectmanagement	eSCM
ISPL	DSDM/Atern	IACCM
IT4IT®	ICB / NCB	ISA-95
IT-CMF™	ISO 21500	ISO 9000/9001
IT Service CMM	MINCE®	OPBOK
ITIL®	M_o_R®	SixSigma
MOF	MSP®	SOX
MSF	P3O®	SqEME®
SABSA	PMBOK® Guide	
SAF	Praxis®	
SIAM™	PRINCE2®	
TRIM		
VeriSM™		
XLA®		

For the latest information on VHP publications, visit our website: www.vanharen.net.

THE HARMONY PROJECT WITH P3.EXPRESS

A novel about minimalistic project management

Alexei Kuvshinnikov

Copyright © Van Haren Publishing

Alexei Kuvshinnikov asserts the moral right to be identified as the author of this work in accordance with the Austrian Federal Law on Copyright for Works of Literature and Art and Related Protective Rights (Bundesgesetz über das Urheberrecht an Werken der Literatur und der Kunst und über verwandte Schutzrechte (Urheberrechtsgesetz))

This book uses concepts based on the P3.express guide licensed under CC BY 4.0 (https://P3.express) and the project example "Artophile Centre" licensed under CC BY 4.0 (https:// p3.express/ training/ artophile-center/). The manuscript was reviewed by the P3.express consortium.

All rights reserved. No part of this publication may be reproduced, stored in a retrieval system, or transmitted in any form or by any means, electronic, mechanical, photocopying, recording, or otherwise, without prior written permission of the publisher, nor be otherwise circulated in any form of binding or cover other than that in which it is published and without similar condition being imposed on the subsequent purchaser.

ISBN paperback: 9789401810548
ISBN eBook: 9789401810555
ISBN ePub: 9789401810562

All characters and events in this publication are fictitious and any resemblance to actual persons, living or dead, is purely coincidental.

I owe so much to so many.
For family, friends and colleagues, present and absent.

Contents

A01 - Appoint the sponsor 3

A02 - Appoint the project manager 9

A03 - Appoint the key team members 18

A04 - Describe the project 46

A05 - Identify and plan the deliverables 68

A06 - Identify risks and plan responses 93

A07 – Have project initiation peer reviewed 103

A08 - Take a go/no-go decision 117

A09 – Kick off the project 124

A10 - Conduct a focused communication 140

B01 - Revise and refine the plans 145

B02 - Have the monthly cycle peer-reviewed 156

B03 - Make a go/no-go decision 163

B04 - Kick-off the monthly cycle 171

B05 - Conduct a focused communication 178

C01 - Measure and report performance 181

C02 - Plan responses for deviations 184

C03 - Kick off the weekly cycle 186

C04 - Conduct a focused communication 190

D01 - Manage risks, issues and change requests 195

D02 - Accept completed deliverables 197

E01 - Evaluate stakeholder satisfaction 215

E02 - Capturing lessons and planning for responses...217

E03 - Conduct a focused communication......................220

F01 - Hand over the product...225

F02 - Evaluate stakeholder satisfaction..........................229

F03 - Have the closing activity group peer reviewed...230

F04 - Archive the project documentation......................231

F05 - Celebrate!..233

F06 - Conduct a focused communication 235

G01 - Evaluate the benefits 239

G02 - Generate new ideas...242

G03 - Conduct a focused communication.....................244

Project Initiation

A01 — Appoint the sponsor
A02 — Appoint the project manager
A03 — Appoint the key team members
A04 — Describe the project
A05 — Identify and plan the deliverables
A06 — Identify risks and plan responses
A07 — Have project initiation peer-reviewed
A08 — Take a go/no-go decision
A09 — Kick off the project
A10 — Conduct a focused communication

A01 - Appoint the sponsor

THE CLOCK AT the top of the Grand Bell Tower struck midnight. The bass rumble of the ancient bell resonated through the quiet streets. Standing at the top of the shallow steps, Didi took in the nightscape. The Grand Concourse that led from the Place Etoile with the belltower in the middle all the way to the Monteith Palace stretched across, all but empty of cars. Late spring air smelt fresh and frosty. It felt like nirvana after spending the day – another day – locked in the office.

Through the transparent trellis of leafless tree branches, Didi could observe a tight knot of people huddling at the stairs that descended to the underground entrance of the Metro station. All were wearing baggy hoodies that concealed their figures. Deep in the black ovals framed by the hoods, cigarettes glowed like a predators' eye.

Didi's mobile phone chimed announcing an incoming call. 'Hello, Didi, this is Rilke's Chief of Office. I apologise for such a late call but access records suggest that you are still somewhere rather close to the office.'

Rilke was the CEO of Artophyle Inc., and Didi, employed in a position that was as good as invisible to the upper management tiers. No wonder then that Didi felt surprised, annoyed and intrigued by the call, all at once. 'You are right, Chief, - I'm standing on the steps just outside of the vestibule.'

Before proceeding to ask what the matter was, Didi had the presence of mind to bite the tongue. It made better sense not to show any interest in what was going on. Though whatever it was, it did seem to exude a whiff of adventure.

'Right,' the Chief continued in a mildly apologetic voice. 'The boss would like to have a chat with you on the phone. Just a quickie of your goodness, if that's not asking too much.'

'Sure.' Didi was getting a bit wary of all that small talk. True, Artophyle ran in a generally democratic way, but summons from the boss rarely included this kind of a prelude, regardless. After a moment's silence, Didi heard Rilke's voice speaking in familiar clipped sentences.

'I hope you're keeping well, Didi. It's good that I could speak to you now. I'm on my way to the airport. Let's talk on the way and my driver will then deliver you home.'

The Chief came back on line. 'Just stay where you are Didi. Or better still, please go down to the driveway at the foot of the stairs. We'll be right there in no time at all.'

Didi started descending the stairs. On the Grand Concourse, three police cruisers swept out of the shadows like night owls. In the time it took Didi to go down half a dozen steps, they glided to an abrupt stop in front of the huddled hoodies. Eight cops jumped out, guns drawn and lined up on the group. Using red laser-sighting lines like virtual whips, the cops herded the hoodies even tighter together.

The Grand Concourse and central districts of Artopolis located north of the river had a dynamic police presence that held street crime mostly at bay. South of the river, where Didi rented a cubicle apartment in a high-rise cluster, was more like Gotham City. You had to watch where you trod or risk somebody putting the leather to you.

A police van arrived in a halo of flashing strobe lights accompanied by a siren wail. The hoodies climbed aboard, seemingly offering only token resistance. Didi reached the bottom of the stairs. Doors slammed, engines roared, lights flashed, sirens barked and howled and the police cavalcade took off. About five seconds later, the boss's sleek black limo glided to a stop right in front. Didi got momentarily mole-eyed, blinded by the glare from street lights reflected in its highly polished curves.

The middle door opened and the Chief beckoned Didi from the inside. Rilke sat on the divan in the back, looking a bit dwarfed by the opulence of the limousine's fittings. And tired. The Chief pointed to a rotating chair that faced the boss at an angle from a distance of some three metres. Didi sat and at once felt anchored to the cushions. The limo smoothly picked up speed. Fleeting stripes of illumination flickered across Rilke's face, leaving it most of the time in dusky shadow.

Rilke's gaze roamed the space inside the car and finally locked on Didi like twin cannons behind telescope-grade lenses. 'I wanted to speak to you, Didi, on a matter of pressing importance.'

Didi guessed that the circumstances promised more carrot than stick and ventured to move a bar forward in their verbal menuetto. 'Is there any way I can be of help?'

Rilke nodded several times, with the cannons' sights remaining locked on Didi. 'I've just got the green light from Schwartz, you know, the Chairman of the Board of ArtoHolding, to embark on a project of strategic importance. No, that's an understatement. You see, Schwartz told me in no uncertain terms what precisely we must deliver. As you'll imagine, failure would yield deeply unpleasant outcomes.'

Didi felt strangely calm. Rilke represented the absolute boundary of Didi's world. Anything and anyone beyond the boss existed in outer space.

Rilke seemed to wait for Didi's reaction and observing none, chuckled in quiet delight. 'You see, ArtoHolding submitted a bid to host the quadrennial Save the Planet Award ceremony. That's the ultimate get-together of the world's celebrities. And you know what?' Rilke grinned and raised shoulders making a palms-up gesture. 'ArtoHolding has been awarded the honour! And now Schwartz wants Artophyle to take the lead and build the new convention centre to serve as the ceremony's venue, right here in Artopolis. Can you imagine that?'

Didi didn't know for sure, so decided to adopt an elusive stance. 'I suppose money is not an issue then?'

Rilke grinned again. 'You are spot on, Didi. The Artopolis mayor has invested a large amount – 4,200 artopools to be exact - in preparing the city for this cosmic event. Part of this fund has been earmarked to cover a share of the costs of our construction project. By the way, I decided to call it the 'Halls of Harmony Project', or HAHAP for short. Though for company visibility purposes we'll call the convention centre Artophyle Halls of Harmony.' Rilke's face radiated an innocent smile. 'Or maybe we should abbreviate it to AHHA?'

Didi pretended to not notice the quip and instead decided to push a bit. 'I suppose then there are some strings attached, aren't there?'

Rilke seemed to hesitate on how to react but finally decided to offer another friendly grin. 'Ah, you are so sharp, Didi. Indeed, indeed, after hosting the award ceremony we'll occasionally make the convention centre available to the mayor at no charge for holding their own events. But that is fully in line with our broader policy aimed to support community interests.

'Most of the time we'll let artistic, cultural, and not-for-profit event organisers use it for free. And if any slots remain free, we could fill them with our own events. The latter will add to the promotion of our community focus and public image.

'And last but not least, we'll occasionally rent it out to other businesses to generate a bit of revenue and recover the project cost. All in all, I hope we'll get great visibility and spread our name in the market as a leading architectural firm.'

The limo sped along the Airport Expressway and Didi decided it was high time to go for the jugular. 'So, if you don't mind my asking, is there an overall idea of what the budget and project duration will actually look like?'

Rilke got a bit pensive and for a minute or so focused his gaze on the starlit sky above the limo's glass roof before returning it to Didi. 'The ceremony is scheduled to take place in twenty-eight months. Accordingly, we better aim to have it ready in twenty-four months, plus a two-month time tolerance on top of that. Regarding the cost, I'll set the initial budget at some 1000 artopools. We can talk about cost tolerance during project initiation.'

Didi smelt a rat. 'Sorry to interrupt, but could I ask you to clarify what you mean when you say -we-?'

Rilke stopped the flow of discourse in midsentence, looking a bit peeved by such a blatant display of insubordination. 'I mean several things. The first of them being, I am in charge.'

A02 - Appoint the project manager

THE LIMO STOPPED at the checkpoint to get admission to the General Aviation part of the airport apron, where Rilke's executive jet stood under steam. Didi became acutely aware that the deep purpose of this hurriedly set up and largely chance conversation remained absolutely unclear. And only minutes remained to figure that out. 'So, how do I fit into your plans?'

Rilke seemed almost surprised by the fact the ride was nearly over. 'Oh, right - I am told you are a diligent project manager, reliable and capable. Accordingly, I appoint you as HAHAP's project manager.'

For a moment, Didi was struck speechless. 'Wow, thank you, that's a fantastic opportunity for me. I really appreciate your trust in my abilities.'

'Good. I'm counting on you, Didi. The Chief will see to it that your appointment is announced first thing in the morning.

You'll report directly to me and I'll take all decisions. We are in the same boat now, Didi, with Schwartz holding the sword over our heads. It will be a job of a work, but we'll manage.'

The car pulled to a stop beside a late-model Gulfstream in a charcoal grey livery with emerald accents. Didi summoned up courage and spoke in a voice, coarse with anxiety. 'With all respect, that won't work.'

The flight attendant had already opened the limo door and Rilke had one foot planted on the tarmac, ready to step out. 'What was that? No, I mean, what do you mean? I told you how we'll work together and I am not interested in your opinions.'

Didi decided it was too late for backtracking, literally. It was going on two o'clock in the morning, the ride back would take another hour or so. The prospect of three hours' sleep before another gruelling commute and an exhausting day in the office made Didi lose the fear. In for a penny, in for a pound. 'You said, we were in the same boat. If we do like you say, the boat will surely sink and pull me under. I don't know how you'll feel about that but personally, I have no intention of letting it get that far. Thank you for the offer, but I'm climbing out. Out of the boat, I mean.'

Rilke remained frozen with one leg on the tarmac and the body unnaturally twisted on the seat. The Chief turned away, instantly mesmerised by the tableau of twinkling airport lights that could be observed through the limo's side window.

With as good as nothing to lose, Didi decided to up the stakes and unloaded another broadside. 'In Artophyle, we run projects using a method called P3.express. It sets down some clear rules and establishes a structure of roles and responsibilities. That's one reason our projects are successful. Well, mostly, but that's not the point I'm trying to make. What you propose will violate that approach and reduce the chances of the project's success.'

Rilke completed the turn and planted the second foot on the tarmac. The head, however, not unlike a tank turret, remained facing in Didi's direction. 'Do you have any kind of ID on you?'

That threw Didi completely. 'Sure, my company ID and my police ID, too. Why?'

'Do you keep a pet?'

Didi's confusion only deepened. 'No.'

'Then you fly with me. We'll talk more in the air.' Rilke climbed out of the car and spoke across the limo roof to the Chief who got out a whole second earlier. 'Get Didi's passport shipped to our destination by overnight courier.'

As soon as their small party had climbed aboard and taken their seats, the steps were retracted, the door closed and engines started. Inside ten minutes the Gulfstream was airborne and climbing steeply to its initial cruising altitude of 45,000 feet.

* * *

After take-off, Rilke had declared a truce until the morning to rest and get ready for the day ahead, which carried a promise of tiring exploits. Rilke's sleeping quarters were up front. Didi was shown to a narrow but sufficiently comfortable berth aft. With engines humming right outside and stuff rattling and tinkling in the nearby galley, this was the

Gulfstream equivalent of economy class. Didi didn't mind at all.

Didi's head spun for a while from the snowballing of the night's events that seemed hardly real. Barely three hours back, Didi had been standing on the office steps trying to figure out how to slip into the Metro without drawing the hoodies' undue attention. And now, Didi was cruising high above the sleeping world to a still unknown destination in the executive jet, without as much as a tooth brush for baggage. Then sleep came like a wave.

When the attendant gently woke Didi, the cabin was already awash in brilliant sunlight. The sky was a deep, rich blue, the curvature of the earth being discernible in the bowlike configuration of fluffy clouds stretching across the horizon. Below the clouds, the greenish calm seas glittered in the sun. After completing morning ablutions, only slightly truncated by the jet's spatial constraints, Didi rummaged through the galley, pouring a cup of freshly brewed coffee and happily attacking a plate of scrambled eggs and fried bacon.

The divider curtain parted in the middle and the Chief's head emerged, beckoning Didi with a nod. Up in the forward lounge, Rilke waited for them sipping coffee, already formally dressed in anticipation of their arrival. 'And a very good morning to you Didi. I hope you feel rested and energised with what the day has in store for you.'

Didi's heart missed a beat. 'And what would that be? I mean, broadly speaking?'

Rilke affected a fatherly mood. 'Oh, mostly adventure and discovery. Meeting highly talented people. Tasting some jolly good food. Possibly even enjoying some top-grade entertainment. Welcome to the executive's life!'

This time Rilke didn't only grin but burst into laughter with sincerity and abandon. The Chief quickly joined in and after a moment's hesitation, Didi felt swept away by such good spirits, too.

As quickly as erupting in laughter, Rilke regained composure and looked sternly at Didi from under a furrowed forehead. 'But before we land and the fun starts, let's sort out this thing with P3.express. I didn't understand from Adam what you said yesterday. Tell me more about it. I want to be educated.'

Didi sat upright, straightening the back to radiate more competence. 'P3.express is a minimalist project management system. It includes ten steps during project initiation, five steps in monthly initiation, four steps for weekly management, two steps for daily management, three steps for monthly closure, six steps for project closure and three steps in post-project management.'

Rilke interrupted by raising a hand. 'That's too much detail. Give it to me in broad brush.'

Didi regrouped. 'Before we can start project delivery, we need to find our way through project initiation. The go/no-go decision will depend on the feasibility of the project plan including a schedule. But before we can prepare a plan, we need to prepare the project description. And that will include also a detailed identification of deliverables.

'The project manager can't be always expected to know enough about the technical aspects of the projects to identify the complete breakdown structure of deliverables on their own. That's one reason for assembling the project team first, to ensure that the project manager has easy access to technical expertise.

'But assembling the cross-departmental project team requires organisational leverage and authority that the project manager won't have. As a consequence, the very first step will be the appointment of the project sponsor.'

With a pensive chew of the upper lip, Rilke stood the ground. 'But that's what I decided yesterday, didn't I? I'll take on the role of the sponsor. What's wrong with that?'

Didi didn't break stride. 'There's plenty wrong with that. The project manager leads a management team whose composition depends on the size and complexity of the project. The project manager is responsible for project delivery and reports to the internal sponsor. The latter is a senior manager accountable for the final outcome of the project by making high-level decisions and delegating the day-to-day running of the project to the project manager.

Rilke looked like working up a snit. 'That's precisely what I told you yesterday, or are you scheming to fob me off?'

Didi sighed and counted until five before continuing. 'Yesterday you told me that you'll tell me what to do and I'll be your eager beaver. That's not quite the same what I'm trying to explain to you now. The project manager should be allowed to do the day-to-day running of the project within the agreed limits of delegated authority without interference from the sponsor. No micro-management. It's the project manager who determines when to involve the sponsor in decision-taking.

'The sponsor's role is necessary because, on the one hand, the project manager has to focus on the day-to-day work and the outputs of the project, which won't leave them enough time and mental energy to manage the high-level aspects of the project. And on the other, the project manager won't have enough organisational clout to be able to get resources for the project, or to have access to strategic information to make sure that the project is aligned with other organisational endeavours.

'The sponsor should be accessible to the project manager for providing guidance and advice at all times. There is no way the sponsor will tell the project manager "Hold on, I'll get back to you when I have a spare moment". And the sponsor is accountable for project success. Or failure.

'If you care to listen to my humble opinion, you are too busy with your CEO responsibilities and I'm not sure you are ready to incur the wrath of Schwartz in case things don't go quite as planned. And on such a project – as a matter of fact, on any project – they almost inevitably do.'

As if on cue, the plane's wheels smoothly connected with the runway. When the plane slowed and veered off to the taxiway, Rilke looked at Didi with a gun-turret stare. 'I appreciate your directness, Didi. That's one reason why I believe you're a good project manager and have a growing certainty that my choice of you was wise, indeed. Now, read my lips: I'll be the project sponsor. Sorted.'

* * *

The plane taxied to the remote part of the airport apron reserved for general aviation. The attendant opened the door, and a gust of hot air heavily laced with the stench of aviation kerosene and the pungent scent of jet exhaust gushed into the cabin.

Didi didn't have a clue where in the world they were. Knowing that it took them some six-seven hours of flying time from Artopolis didn't help much without knowing in which direction they had gone. Since neither Rilke nor the Chief had volunteered to reveal their destination, Didi decided it was prudent not to ask them questions to this end. May be, need-to-know applied.

A beige limousine with mirrored windows glided to a halt at the foot of the aircraft stair. A chase car - white square-looking SUV - followed it closely. Its intended menacing appearance was enhanced by a chrome-plated bullbar. The small convoy sped through the checkpoint in the airport fence without stopping. Didi's puny collection of IDs remained untouched.

They drove quickly along a cracked and patched two-way road mostly devoid of traffic going in either direction. Tall palms with lush fronds ran along both shoulders of the road. They skirted a medium-sized low-slung town with a mammoth water tank in the centre rising on its spindly legs like an alien war machine from *The War of the Worlds*.

Since the beige limousine was two sizes smaller than Rilke's own executive ride, Didi sat squeezed up front next to the driver. The seat was spartan, the legroom lacking and on top of that, the driver concentrated on the traffic and offered no conversation.

Still, Didi saw an opportunity to satisfy the itching curiosity and managed to land one question. 'Where in the world are we?'

The driver condescended and broke the code of silence. 'We're some fifteen miles away from Zourbagan, the capital city of the Republic of Sanriol, moving at an average speed of sixty-five miles per hour in a south-easterly direction. ETA at destination in twenty-three minutes.'

As that exhausting answer precluded any follow-on question, Didi focused instead on taking stock of the situation and planning the next moves.

Buying some clothes and a pair of sneakers took absolute priority. The charcoal business suit definitely looked out of place there. Next on the list was advancing project initiation.

Activity A01 focused on the appointment of the sponsor. That had been taken care of and the next days would show if it were for the better or the worse.

Activity A02 – appointment of the project manager – could also be ticked off.

Next in line was Activity A03 – appointment of key project team members.

A03 - Appoint the key team members

COMPOSITION OF the project team depended to a large degree on the project product. HAHAP aimed to produce a huge conference centre. Accordingly, Didi immediately thought of a marketing wizard to help with the business aspects of the project and a designer to lead the architectural aspects. Their handlers would be respectively Anan, director of the sales and marketing department, and Imani, director of the design department.

In Didi's experience, getting staff assigned to the project team proved inevitably an uphill struggle. Department heads used every trick they knew to avoid the actual secondment of their employees to project teams. They hated losing control over their workhorses.

The favourite ruse was to promise that department staff would be available to respond to any specific requests from the project manager, while at the same time remaining in the firm grasp of department heads who kept the last say on what was the department's top priority and what wasn't. Predictably, project requirements were assigned the lowest priority, for which department specialists never had any time left. And the project manager had no means of challenging departmental heads about their decisions. They were on their home turf.

At that juncture, the sponsor's superior firepower came in very handy. The project sponsor thus had a key role in assembling the project team, negotiating with departments to appoint their staff to the team, bringing them under the project manager's line of command. That was one reason the sponsor was needed at all - to fight stratospheric battles of influences. Didi had little doubt that Rilke could decimate any managerial obstruction with absolute ease. The question was, rather, if the boss could be sufficiently impressed with the importance and urgency of engaging in what to Rilke were only petty skirmishes.

The cars left the main road at an unmarked exit, entering under a canopy formed by manicured palms, passing under an elaborate arch overgrown with flowering bougainvillea that welcomed them to paradise. The limo crunched over a gravel drive and pulled up in front of what looked like a hugely oversized Bahamian clapboard house. A small army of valets, bell boys and receptionists swarmed out to greet Rilke.

In the ensuing commotion, Didi succeeded in commandeering Rilke's attention. 'Boss, could you please tell Anan and Imani to assign a sales and marketing expert and a design expert to the project team to support me in the formulation of the project description. That's rather urgent, I'm afraid.'

Rilke waved Didi away like a midge. 'Talk to the Chief to fix that. But there is no rush, this time zone is some five hours ahead of Artopolis, which plays into our hands. I've got a full day's schedule of meetings and lunches. While I'm labouring through it, feel free to enjoy the amenities. This is a truly fabulous place. And in the evening, let's meet in the terrace bar and have a chat.'

Three hours later, Didi sat munching on a bunch of small red bananas in an easy chair on the room's balcony that overlooked a grove of palms. A sortie into a nearby town had yielded some basic stuff to wear and an equally basic notebook that was nevertheless perfectly fit for purpose. Living the high-life felt good.

Didi promptly set up the new project in a separate directory on a dedicated Artophyle cloud server hosted on a secure and privacy-aware platform, complemented by a team chat. Appointment of the initial project team members being still pending didn't present an obstacle to starting the drafting of the project description.

In a nutshell, it included the project name, project purpose, expected cost and duration, requirements and quality expectations regarding the project product, a high-level description of in-scope and out-of-scope elements and a list of stakeholders.

A cornerstone of P3.express was the incremental approach to all project management activities, be it outputs or project documentation. Project initiation involved preparing, getting the sponsor's approval and baselining of the first version of the project description.

It didn't prevent the project manager at all from revising and updating different elements of the project descriptions with new information obtained later, during project delivery. The project description, like any other document in P3.express, was a living document.

Concerning the project name, Rilke had already chosen it – The Halls of Harmony Project, or HAHAP. All in all, the higher level of management had the prerogative to decide on the project name to ensure they connected with the organisation's portfolio.

Description of the project purpose also included a review of its expected benefits or, in their absence, outcomes. This distinction described a subtle but important nuance. The responsibility for determining benefits corresponded to the higher-level organisational level, like programme management, rather than the project team. The latter could only propose project outcomes for the sponsor's consideration.

In the case of HAHAP, Rilke had expressed the corporate vision of benefits rather clearly.

- Promoting the company.
- Engaging with the mayor.
- Engaging with the community.
- Obtaining revenue from commercial leases.
- Having a convenient place for their own events.

Rilke's current estimate of cost and duration stood at respectively 1000 artopools and twenty-four months. Didi didn't have a clue how realistic that rough executive estimate was but, following the incremental approach, more precise information would be gleaned in the later course of project initiation.

Project product requirements described the functionality expected from the sum of the deliverables. The project description also included quality expectations related to the project product. But, since both of these elements were expected to be highly technical, it was the project team and not solely the project manager who would define them.

The same criterion applied to the production of high-level description of in-scope and out-of-scope elements of the project product. These would be determined during workshops conducted with the participation of project team members and a broader selection of in-house experts.

The initial list of stakeholders included:

- Rilke: CEO, project sponsor
- Didi: project manager
- Schwartz: Chairman of the Board, ArtoHolding
- Anan: director of the sales and marketing department
- Imani: director of the design dep…

* * *

…Didi woke up with a jerk three hours later, slowly realising the mean joke played by the jetlag. One moment Didi was fully awake, and the next, sound asleep, knocked out cold for most of the afternoon.

The room phone gave a mellow ring. 'Cheers, Didi, this is the Chief speaking. The boss is running late, I'm afraid, and besides our hosts decided to offer a social event tonight. So, don't bet your paycheque on meeting Rilke tonight.'

Somehow, Didi wasn't particularly surprised. 'Chief, did you manage to speak to Anan and Imani regarding the appointment of their reps to the project team?'

In response, silence.

'Chief? Are you there?'

The Chief came back in a hurried voice. 'Sorry, Didi, Rilke is dragging me to yet another meeting. No, I couldn't call them as I spend the whole time live with the boss. But I've texted them.'

'Any response yet'?

'I'll let you know the moment I get any.'

It took quite some effort to believe that a texted request from the Chief would not be actioned immediately and the confirmation of action taken texted back. Which meant that, in all probability, the Chief was not fully sincere. And Didi had never been inclined to let anyone get away with a bald-faced lie.

'Hey Chief, it seems to me that in the last twenty-four hours office, discipline went into a nose-dive. When the cat's away, the mice will play."

'Indeed, indeed. Trust me, they are up for a whipping when we get back. Sorry, need to end this call now. Cheers.' The Chief hung up, a tad too hurriedly in Didi's considered opinion.

In a flash of inspiration, Didi went to the digital edition of *The Sanriol Gazette*. Nothing of interest in the headlines but, scanning the business section, Didi noticed a piece titled 'Artophyle CEO arrives in own jet, receives a red-carpet welcome'.

Reading the article, Didi learned that Artophyle Inc. was one of the world's most renowned. in demand architectural design companies and prospective clients regarded joining the small club of its customers as a great honour. The piece further portrayed Rilke as a business guru and top-notch design visionary.

Rilke had arrived in response to the invitation from the local association of corporate bankers with the objective of discussing the envisaged attractions of taking on the designing and construction of a new financial district in the capital, Zourbagan. The government had reached a preliminary endorsement from the Global Development Bank on the subject of a loan to finance the cost of the eventual contract, estimated to be in the nine-digit league.

According to *The Sanriol Gazette*, Rilke's visit had started with an audience with the honourable prime minister of Sanriol. The board of governors of the local association of corporate bankers had him next. And for lunch, the star CEO had the local director of the above-mentioned Global Development Bank.

A tour of the capital city of Zourbagan filled the afternoon programme. At night, Rilke and the prime minister were awaited at a cocktail reception offered in their honour by corporate bankers, preceded by a jazz and reggae extravaganza by famous local performers.

Didi felt a pang of envy. Rubbing elbows with the prime minister and the banker cohort didn't seem like a particularly enticing way of passing the evening. But jazz and reggae were a different kettle of fish.

The article changed Didi's perception of the relative importance that HAHAP had for Artophyle. Sure, it could draw lots of visibility. Sure, it could conceivably do marvels for promoting Artophyle to the world. It absolutely would reinforce their relationship with the mayor of Artopolis and possibly allow a degree of access to the political influences enjoyed by the mayor's party. All good. But it remained more of a prestige project than a money-making one.

Whatever its expected benefits, they definitely paled before the prospect of signing a contract for the new Zourbagan financial district with a revenue expectation that dwarfed that of HAHAP. That was where Artophyle and ArtoHolding would focus their attention and resources.

A separate activity in the project initiation focused on risk identification. But it made sense to begin recording risks as they surfaced.

Didi knew from experience that revenue-generating projects funded by external clients inevitably got priority over internally funded ones. As Artophyle was hardly a big company, on most occasions it had to share its finite resources among multiple projects. Obviously enough, it spawned competition for the limited resources and projects set up to generate revenue from external financing and requiring only in-kind contributions from Artophyle without tying up its smallish capital reserves understandably got higher priority.

So, if HAHAP had to compete for resources with the financial district project, from the perspective of the former, there was a significant risk that preference would be given to the latter.

That observation led to another. HAHAP already suffered from competition for resources. The financial district project had commandeered all of Rilke' time while pushing Didi's own requirements to the back-burner.

Rilke's decision to become the project sponsor was flawed. That much seemed perfectly clear now. But Didi couldn't do anything much about it at the moment. Didi could only dare to confront Rilke and attempt the arm-twisting using damning evidence. And there was none.

The problem became clear, and the solution equally so. Didi started building a case.

* * *

Another attempt to get the Chief on the phone predictably brought no result. Didi then texted the Chief regarding the appointment of staff from Anan's and Imani's department to the project team, making it clear that it had become a pressing issue.

Didi pondered the situation a bit more. HAHAP was starting off on the wrong foot, no doubt about it. This realisation demanded a proactive approach. Didi set up the follow-up register and recorded the issues that had become evident in the last hour or so.

ID: I-001

Cause: CEO took on the role of the sponsor.

Effect: As HAHAP has lower priority than the financial district project, the sponsor does not address HAHAP requirements quickly enough.

Impact: High-level decisions are delayed causing knock-on delays in project initiation.

Response: Collecting evidence to present it to the sponsor.
Custodian: Didi
Status: Open

ID: I-002

Cause: the sponsor not responding to project manager's requests to achieve the appointment of staff from the sales/marketing and design departments to the project team.

Effect: Formulation of project description, identification and planning of deliverables, identification of risks and planning responses delayed.

Impact: Go/No-go decision delayed causing project slippage.

Response: Persistently sending reminders regarding pending decisions.

Custodian: Didi
Status: Open

Having checked if there were any messages from the Chief – there were none - Didi then went for a stroll in the palm grove. Following only the briefest twilight, a tropical night had already descended. The paths were rather poorly lit and impenetrable darkness shrouded most of the gardens. Palm fronds rustled in the light breeze, their movement occasionally making the invisible tree trunks bend and creak in the night.

A strong odour of packed dirt, dried vegetation and rotting fruit rose from the undergrowth. Some kind of small animals – or reptiles? – rustled in the brushwood. From the palm fronds, screeching bird cries pierced the night. Or maybe those were the fear-inspiring flying foxes?

Didi had anticipated a stroll in more romantic and peaceful surroundings and quickly got unnerved by the wild-sounding and evil-smelling jungle that enfolded the paths. For a city-dweller from another hemisphere, the overall atmosphere felt eerie and even a tad unsettling.

Back in the residence, Didi found a platter of club sandwiches and a small bowl with fruit placed on the room console. Nice! In improved spirits, Didi happily munched on the simple but tasty and obviously freshly-made fare. Didi then checked the phone (no calls or messages), took a long shower, checked the phone (nothing), fell onto the bed and was asleep before hitting the pillow. No dreams came.

* * *

The morning broke like the first morning. Still in bed, Didi checked the phone. Nothing. This kind of disregard called for a reaction.

Breakfast was served on the ground-floor terrace with steps leading onto a manicured lawn. At that hour of the morning, shortly after six, the terrace was deserted, which played perfectly into Didi's hands. Time passed slowly. The breakfast being modelled in the English tradition, Didi unhurriedly went through its numerous mandatory elements.

Rilke appeared shortly before eight, impeccably dressed and looking without a care in the world, dragging the slightly dishevelled-looking Chief in tow. Seeing Didi, Rilke momentarily slowed the brisk pace, as if surprised by such an encounter, but instantly recovered. 'Good morning, Didi. How are you doing today? Could I beg you to join me if not for breakfast - I can see that you've been toiling at it for quite a while - than at least for a chat.'

'Good morning, boss.' Didi was all warmth and smiles. 'How did yesterday go?'

Rilke turned the opening tepid smile up a few degrees. 'Oh, smashing, absolutely terrific. Fantastic reception all the way, an audience with the prime minister, a marvellous lunch and an amazing social event that lasted into the wee small hours. I'm positively feeling energised.'

Didi matched the warmth of Rilke's smile and then raised the stakes some more. 'Did you by any chance manage to address my request?'

Rilke's smile cooled perceptibly. 'I told you that the chief would take care of it, didn't I?'

Didi nodded enthusiastically. 'As a matter of fact, you did. But you see, boss, it's you who are the sponsor of HAHAP, not the chief. You can delegate your responsibilities to a proxy, but not the accountability for the results.'

Rilke turned the guns on the Chief. 'Can we get it sorted, now?'

The Chief fiddled with the starched napkin avoiding eye contact with Rilke. 'It's now 3:12 a.m. in Artopolis.'

'Right,' Rilke slowly worked his anger up, looking for the direction in which to blow the top off. 'Why didn't you talk to Anan and Imani yesterday?'

The Chief knew the boss. They went back together a long way. 'You told me to stay by your side at all times, never leaving you alone, be it even for a moment. I had to ask your generous permission to go to the bloody bathroom. And your directive had a good reason, too. Because you have too much mouth, Boss. You needed me to feed you background, smooth out the impact of the nonsense you babbled, put you back on tracks when you went off them and last but not least…'

Rilke raised both hands in mock surrender and merrily laughed. The anger was gone. 'Getting brave'n'lippy, aren't we, Chief? I know I'd be as good as lost without you. But don't stretch it too much, eh?'

Rilke suddenly whipped around to face Didi. 'Same goes for you, understood? I like directness, but only to a point. Don't ever try to make me the villain of the piece. You'll have to get used to my way of doing things and my pace. If I prefer to delegate or communicate with you through a proxy, that's my conscious choice and it's up to you to figure out how to make it work for you.'

Didi nodded without uttering a word. The prime minister's aide de camp spilt onto the terrace in a flurry of motion. 'Pardon me, sir, but the skipper would appreciate receiving you immediately.'

Rilke uttered a mild obscenity under the breath and rose from the table. The Chief scurried after, casting Didi a helpless and apologetic glance.

Didi remained unperturbed by all the theatrics and calmly finished the third cup of fragrant morning tea. 'Now, now, in Hamlet's words, something's rotten in the State of Denmark, no offense to the Danes.'

Another person appeared on the terrace, moving with the unhurried and confident gait of an athlete. Or a bodyguard. 'Morning Didi. My name's Mo. I'm skipper's junior minder. Since your boss will be tied up in meetings much of the day, I've been detailed as your host and guide. Our destination for today is a range of extinct volcanoes that's truly a visiting card of Sanriol.'

Didi went back to the room to change and briefly surf the web for an update about the advance of Rilke's charm offensive. This time the choice fell on the blog of an opposition activist. It painted a somewhat bleaker picture of yesterday's events.

The fanfare surrounding the visit of the Artophyle CEO presumably attempted to obscure the gaping difference in the views of the ruling party, as expressed by the prime minister and the association of corporate bankers ruled by his cronies on the one hand, and the Global Development Bank on the other.

The former wanted the future financial district to rise as an architectural landmark of global impact to rank somewhere between the Burj Khalifa and the Warisan Merdeka Tower.

The latter insisted on a neutral carbon imprint, top-notch energy efficiency, use of renewable sources of energy, reduction of water waste and implementing climate-smart architecture in conjunction with nurturing forest landscapes. The last criterion produced a particularly nasty contradiction with the vision of a 680-metre tower.

The opposition gave full backing to the conditions imposed by the Global Development Bank, perhaps because of its sudden soft spot for fighting climate change, but mostly due to its natural desire to throw a spanner in the government's works at every opportunity.

Both camps appeared to have dug in, and the blogger predicted another day of tense and gruelling negotiations.

Mo calmly waited, leaning against the flank of a beige SUV, and courteously opened the door for Didi. Being of an older vintage, the SUV sported more curves than angles, emphasising elegance over brutality. Fastening the seat belt, Didi glanced around and noticed a functional-looking submachine gun with collapsible stock latched to the back of the driver's seat. In response to an inquisitive glance, Mo just gave an indifferent shrug.

They drove with the windows open, as if floating on the strong currents of hot air. On occasions it carried the odour of vegetation rot, on others, the perfume of blooming flowers, steel, and the reek of diesel exhaust fumes from the big lumber trucks they passed. Mo drove competently, fast but never reckless, and looked composed but relaxed behind the steering wheel.

Didi had slipped into the tourist mode with a light heart and felt no qualms at all regarding deserting from work. At that early stage in the project, in a situation when the sponsor was tied up with more pressing issues, there wasn't anything the project manager could do, except be patient. Antagonising the sponsor never paid off for the project manager and nicking the executive could be more dangerous than useful.

Didi knew from experience, paper beats stone. One had only to stay patient and wait for an opening. Tonight might provide one, but more probably, it would be at breakfast time tomorrow when their tussle with Rilke would come to a head. In preparation for the showdown, it made sense to unwind and regain inner balance.

* * *

After some two hours of driving, they made a pit-stop at a decrepit road-side inn. A grizzled wrinkly with gnarled hands served them toasted bread topped with grated tomato and garlic, accompanied by mugs of strong, sweet coffee spiked with zesty cardamom, made by an archaic machine. The owner and the machine, both seemed held together with pieces of frayed string and sheer willpower.

Mo turned off the main road. Soon, the dirt track started climbing through the moist jungle. The track ended at the entrance to a flat meadow with a grange at one side. Two saddled horses grazed up front. In a practised move, Mo slung the machine-gun across the back and went to meet a local in full cowboy attire who stood on the house steps. They shook hands and clapped each other on the shoulder like old buddies.

Mo beckoned Didi, who trailed a few steps back. 'Hey Didi, welcome to the Crater Ranch! Meet the owner and operator of Crater Horseback Tours – my father.' And winked an eye. 'It's only your family that you can trust with really important things.'

Didi stole a cautious glance at the horses. 'Do you mean, we'll actually go riding on horseback? I'd prefer an e-bike.'

'There are no e-bikes here, I'm afraid. There is no juice to charge them.' Mo sounded mischievously apologetic. 'Horses, on the other hand, are equally climate-friendly and easily rechargeable with renewable energy sources. Like oats here.'

After the briefest of briefings, Mo and Didi mounted their horses and set off at an easy trot, following a trail leading up the hill. To say Didi enjoyed the ride would be an overstatement. Fortunately, the horse knew the route and required little intervention from its rider.

First, they rode through a thinning grove of the highest palms Didi had ever seen, fording several shallow creeks that ran down the hillside. Then they entered a copse of prehistoric-looking ferns that rose high above them. Finally, they crossed the tree line, and saw grassland stretching all the way to near the crater lip.

Reaching it, they dismounted, tying the horses to hitching posts. The circular crater measured about a kilometre across. A lake of greenish milky water filled it to some hundred metres under the ridge. Mo seemed to read Didi's thoughts. 'The water rises to about the middle of the crater cone. Plus, there are another fifty metres of sticky mud at its bottom. And there in the mud lie tons of gold and emeralds.'

Didi thought Mo was plying a joke. 'How come?'

Mo smiled mischievously. 'Throwing gold jewellery and gems into the lake was part of a ritual of ascension of zipas, the tribal chiefs. It took place in the mist of times. At least, that's what the legend says.'

Didi absorbed the perfect calm that reigned in the place. It radiated an amazing feeling of being at peace with the nature, the history and one's inner self.

The unmistakeable whup-whup of an approaching helicopter pierced the cocoon of harmony that had enveloped Didi. In one fluid motion, Mo unslung the weapon and held it with its muzzle pointing at the ground, fire selector switched from safety to burst mode.

The helicopter arrived in under a minute, banking sharply over them. It then hovered and quickly sank to a landing on the crater lip some fifty metres away from them, probably not to scare the horses.

Mo must have recognised it as a friendly craft, made the gun safe and slung it back in its usual place. 'It's a special unit machine and apparently, they came for us. Something must have happened. Let's move.'

They jogged the distance, crouching against the rotor blast, and dove inside the copter. The gunny thrust a military-grade flak jacket at Mo and barked a short command to the flight crew. The blades picked up speed, the machine rose and accelerated with the nose pointed down. Mo helped Didi don the body armour, put in place aviator's wrap-around goggles and strapped on the flimsy safety belt. They sat on the side seats gazing into the world unfolding before them through the open slide door. The air rush and engine roar were atrocious.

Next to them, the gunny shifted the pivot-mounted machine gun, scanning the ground beneath them. Mo picked up a headset with a mic arm plugged into the intercom and chatted with the crew. There was another set hanging from a hook at Didi's seat. Following Mo's sign language, Didi put it on and thumbed the listen/talk switch. 'Half an hour ago, the skipper had a close call with a hit squad. There was a shoot-out but it turned out okay. Well, at least relatively so.'

They landed on a helipad on the residence grounds. Didi realised, somewhat belatedly, that this was one of the prime minister's guest houses, which made things a bit clearer. The grounds and the house itself now hosted a modest number of armed characters, dressed as civilians. In a well-rehearsed manner, they went about their chores creating an atmosphere of purpose and competence. Surprisingly, Didi had no sensation of anxiety or of being in acute danger.

Rilke conferred with the Chief and several locals, sipping coffee on the terrace and appearing generally unperturbed. Didi took a seat several tables away and waited for the Boss's summons. In a while, Mo came to say goodbye and Didi offered generous thanks for their trip that had turned out being memorable in more ways than one. Mo gave a salute and went off at a trot to join the security detail.

As Rilke's conference showed no signs of abating, Didi fetched the notebook to while away the time. There was a message from Anan in the inbox.

> Hi Didi, I hope you are keeping well down there in Sanriol. Heard the news about the attack on the Prime Minister's convoy…hardly a tranquil location, isn't it? Coming to the point, the Chief has just called me to tell that the boss appointed me as the sponsor of the 'Halls of Harmony' project, or HAHAP, as it seems to be called. Haven't got a clue what it's about but I suppose you'll explain it when you come back. The Chief has also asked me to appoint somebody from my department to the project team. And also, to talk to Imani to get a designer appointed from their side. From S&M it will then be Sasha. Imani was a bit dodgy and suggested instead to designate someone as a project focal point. I'm not sure it's quite the same thing but again, I suppose it can wait until you get back. Let me know when we can have a chat. Have a safe trip back! Cheers, Anan

Stunned, Didi gazed at the screen in utter amazement that was gradually replaced by a feeling of huge relief. At last, common sense seemed to be prevailing. As Rilke still looked immersed in the conversation, there was time for a short reply.

> Hello Anan, thanks for breaking the news to me. It made me feel really happy! I'll let you know as soon as I'm back, right now waiting for a chat with the Boss who is tied up with local counterparts. Talk to you soon, Didi

Next, Didi updated the two issues that had been captured to the follow-up register.

ID: I-001

Cause: CEO appointed as the sponsor.

Effect: As the HAHAP project has lower priority than the financial district project, the sponsor does not quickly address HAHAP requirements.

Impact: High-level decisions are delayed causing knock-on delays in project initiation.

Response: Collecting information to prove it.

Custodian: Didi.

Status: Closed. Director of sales and marketing department appointed as the project sponsor in the place of the CEO.

ID: I-002

Cause: the sponsor (CEO) not responding to project manager's requests to achieve the appointment of staff from the sales/marketing and design departments to the project team.

Effect: Formulation of project description, identification and planning of deliverables, identification of risks and planning responses delayed.

> **Impact:** Go/No-go decision delayed causing schedule slippage.
>
> **Response:** Sending persistent reminders regarding pending decisions.
>
> **Custodian:** Didi.
>
> **Status:** Closed. The newly appointed project sponsor (Director, S&M) took up contact; communication is dynamic and productive.

Didi felt Rilke's stare and, sure enough, the CEO beckoned the project manager to join them. 'Right, so, where were we now? I've appointed Anan as my replacement in the sponsor role.

'Tonight, I'll be leaving for the Global Development Bank HQ to meet their Chairman of the Board and a few other dignitaries. The financial district project is experiencing some turbulence. Nothing unusual, really, but I'll have to focus on it as it's all about money, and bringing revenue to my shareholders is my primary obligation as the CEO. Since I can't clone myself, you'll have to make do with Anan.

'I was a bit torn between Anan and Imani but decided that the former was a better fit. I felt that while Imani, as the director of the design department, had great knowledge of the technical aspects, Anan, as director of the sales and marketing department, knew most about the project's benefits and their realisation, and that is key for the sponsor's role.

'For management roles it's best to use people who have a focus on the management and business aspects.'

Rilke paused, weighing the next words carefully. 'I'm not sure you know it, Didi, as a matter of fact I doubt you do, but I wasn't born with the executive's silver spoon in my mouth.

'I used to be a technical specialist myself, and in those good old days people with technical knowledge got appointed to lead projects rather often, as project management was still several decades before being recognised as a profession.

'It's not always that I've been a couch potato, either. In my time, I've seen quite some action. I had been what you now would call the sponsor for the project that involved the building of the bridge over river Liss, under enemy fire. And we did build it, didn't we? As a matter of fact, because of the continued artillery and missile damage we had to build it five times.'

'That was way before my watch,' was the only thing Didi could mutter, stunned by Rilke's revelations and the general snowballing of the events.

Rilke grunted with a trace of mild derision. 'Then look it up; you'll be proud of your boss'.

While touched by Rilke's candour, Didi felt it would still be expedient to focus on more pressing things than history. 'Under the circumstances, I suppose it's about time for me to head back to the office.'

Rilke couldn't agree more. 'As I've told you, in a couple of hours, I'm flying to the Global Development Bank HQ. Artopolis lies notably in the opposite direction from here. So, buy yourself a seat on tomorrow's scheduled flight. I'm sure you'll survive the lacking amenities of a budget airline.'

Didi loathed Rilke's sarcasm but saw no sense in showing it. 'Won't be the first time I stand trial by hardship.'

* * *

Waking ap at dawn the next morning, Didi found the residence empty. No boss, no security and, for that matter, seemingly no staff. The breakfast offer included only some cereal, a scrambled egg, fresh fruit and what tasted like yesterday's coffee. It looked like a mock test for flying on a budget fare. But the sun shone, the flowers bloomed and the birds sang in the palm fronds.

Didi read a brief message from Anan, confirming Sasha's appointment to the project team. In another pleasant surprise, Mo showed up in his aged battle cruiser to offer a ride to the airport. A home-made smoked ham and chutney sandwich and tall Styrofoam cup filled with the magic potion from the gnarled inn triggered an outpouring of Didi's ecstatic gratitude. Mo smiled wickedly. 'I kind of know when local hospitality runs out of steam.'

The budget airline fully lived up to its horrendous reputation and the flight proved to be taxing. Back in Artopolis, it was cool, rainy and windy. While the Artophyle finance department considered highly extravagant taxi fare expenses claims, Didi travelled to the cubicle apartment by means of cable car, Metro and tuctuc.

Entering the tiny apartment with the drab cityscape flickering in the dusk outside its small, grimy window, Didi felt dog-tired but at the same time remarkably energised. It was still early evening and high time to set the scene for the next day. Back at the base, Artophyle staff preferred to communicate by texting.

> Hello Anan, I'm back in Artopolis and would dearly love to see you tomorrow. Kindly let me know when you have a free slot in your schedule. Regards, Didi

> Hello Sasha, I'm the project manager of the HAHAP, which is short for the 'Halls of Harmony' project. Anan appointed you to the project team as S&M rep. Let's meet and have a chat tomorrow. Cheers, Didi

* * *

The morning dawned pregnant with rain. The thorny plant in the floor pot looked none the worse for the master's three-day absence. It had seen worse. Much worse. For example, when several years back Didi had spent ten days in the Sisters of Compassion Hospital following a mugging assault one early morning after pulling another all-nighter at the office.

The streets of the neighbourhood pulsed with tuctucs. There, south of the river, they were ubiquitous, appearing in the guises of food trucks, delivery vans, coffee stands and, of course, collectives.

Pushing and deflecting enemy elbows, Didi wiggled through the crowd, waited for the collective that looked marginally less tightly packed than most, grabbed the outside rail with both hands, pulled hard and simultaneously long-jumped, landing on the sideboard. The tuctuc, loaded with double its certified capacity of twelve passengers, perilously tilted to port, but the seasoned driver compensated for the shift in balance and raced on at full throttle, with the wind rushing in Didi's face. The sensation felt not unlike flying in a helicopter over Sanriol. A major difference was the cold wind that stung the cheeks protruding from under the heavy-duty dirt racer's goggles, instead of massaging them.

Leaden clouds clung to the rooftops. The thickset Embankment Towers appeared cut off at the middle. That truncated look made them appear even stouter than they were. They went by the name of Embankment Barrels, a passing tribute to the architectural fiasco they presented. A competitors' fiasco, noted Didi with satisfaction.

The vortex of people rotated around the Loranca Metro station entrance with riders being slowly sucked into its innards. Didi didn't rush in, having a long time ago given a pledge to never go without a decent morning meal. Lunches were a thing of opportunity, and dinners, of happenstance. Given the circumstances, morning meals had become a part of the going-to-work ritual. Artopolis street-food culture that deservedly enjoyed a cult status made it easy.

Didi stopped at a favourite stall and ordered one of the all-time delights – spiced, Asian-style fish soup with grouper steaks and Udon-type noodles. On a cold and windy morning, it did marvels for one's spirits. Slurping the soup and chomping on the juicy fish, Didi exchanged glances and nods with fellow eaters, most complete strangers, in appreciation of the food. That was the camaraderie of people sharing some basic preferences, and all belonging to the same tribe.

Passing by another stall, Didi bought coffee and a jumbo eclair. Now that the gnarled inn in Sanriol had set a standard for coffee, this one tasted a bit flat, but it was still quite passable under the circumstances.

Fortified and in high spirits, Didi felt ready for the daily grind and bravely dove into the human vortex, spreading out the elbows. Inside the cold, damp and gloomy station that offered some functionality but no frills, a packed crowd waited for the train. This line had been built some forty years back, on a lean budget scraped together from bits and pieces and looked as plain as a pikestaff.

Crowds on the platform pulsed in the rhythm set by train intervals. Didi knew how to be patient and was carried aboard the third train. Firmly pressed from all sides and with the soup radiating a pleasant warmth in the stomach, Didi relaxed and swayed with the train's movement. North of the river, the throng in the carriage started gradually thinning, as people alighted to fill gazillion offices. Didi changed trains at Place Etoile, this time riding the few stations east to Maalbek in counterflow, and emerged from the station at a brisk pace, intuitively looking for hoodies that had converged on the entrance – when was it…less than eighty hours ago.

Didi's phone gave a ping, indicating a text message.

> Morning Didi, here is the link to my scheduling app. Pick the slot that suits you best. Cheers, Sasha

Walking up the stairs to the Artophyle haute couture vestibule, Didi looked up the available slots in the scheduling app. Sasha's time for the day was only moderately booked. Didi picked the slot at ten past eleven, adding under the meeting subject:

> Need inputs regarding benefits. I've prepared a draft list on the basis of my conversation with the boss. Please take a look at whether anything is missing or needs refinement.

Still on the go, Didi then plucked the list from cloud storage and dropped it into the message.

Project Description V.0.1 (draft)

Project name: Halls of Harmony (HAHAP)

Benefits (to be discussed and clarified):

- Promoting Artophyle Inc.
- Engaging with the Mayor of Artopolis
- Engaging with the community
- Obtaining revenue from commercial leases
- Having a convenient place for own events

Cost and duration: 1,000 artopools and 24 months.

Tolerances: to be confirmed.

Project product requirements and quality expectations: to be defined.

Stakeholders:

- Anan: sponsor, director of the sales and marketing department
- Didi: project manager
- Schwartz: Chairman of the Board of ArtoHolding
- Rilke: CEO
- Imani: director of the design department

An instant later, Didi received a hit low in the back that knocked him down in a backflip, arms and legs flailing. The phone flew in a steep arc. The rider of an e-roller ably caught it in mid-air on its downward curve and vanished. It all happened within five steps of the vestibule entrance. Didi still had a fraction of a second to make a mental note that the villain sported a baggy soiled-white jumpsuit and wore a blood-red motorcycle helmet with a black visor.

Then came the crash. Didi hit the flagstones sideways with a solid thump that knocked the air out of the lungs and left the head spinning. Stunned colleagues rushed to the rescue. Didi sat up and did damage assessment: probably a hip contusion and bruises along the right side of the body. It hurt, but the incident could have been much worse. With some assistance, Didi managed to stand up and limp through the Artophyle portal to the elevators. Trite as it sounded, texting while walking could be damaging to one's health.

A04 - Describe the project

THE PROJECT management pool occupied an open-plan office space on the seventh floor, with desks arranged in clusters of three. Low partitions made of opaque glass ensured everyone could concentrate on the tasks at hand without the distraction of observing colleagues wildly gesticulating their way through an internet conference.

A lounge area with a fridge, microwave, kettle and a pod coffee machine served as an improvised conference space. Coffee was free, in the expectation of boosting meeting productivity. On the other hand, consumption of energy drinks, while not precisely banned, was stigmatised.

Didi hobbled to the usual desk and fired up the notebook. Concentration helped drive pain away. Activity A03 – Appoint the key team members – barely limped along, while remaining work in progress. On the bright side, Sasha had come on board. On the not-so-bright one, Imani still dragged the feet over appointing the representative of the design department.

Activity A04 with its focus on preparing the project description remained in an embryonic state.

A delicate cough nearby startled Didi, who twisted around in a whirl. 'Oh, that's you Sasha. Sorry, I was on a planning delve.'

Sasha had a compassionate look. 'It's ten past eleven. Are you OK, Didi? I mean, after what has happened this morning. I've heard you had a really nasty fall.'

Didi felt a pang of irritation. 'You bet, but rumours tend to make mountains out of mole hills. I'm mostly OK. Lost my phone, though.'

Sasha frowned with concern. 'Was there anything sensitive, I mean, company-sensitive, on it?'

Now it was Didi's turn to frown, while thinking. 'No, I guess there was nothing, certainly not in terms of texting, if that's what you are hinting at, but it was synchronised with my mailbox. It may be a good idea to change the password.'

Sasha nodded vigorously. 'Absolutely, that's precisely what I mean. And since you've mentioned texting, what about texting the boss while you stayed in Sanriol?'

Didi was suddenly pensive. 'No, we didn't text at all; we just talked.'

Sasha hesitated for several seconds, then decided to press on with the questioning. 'Did you also discuss the particulars of the financial district project?'

'Not the particulars. As a matter of fact, there aren't any yet.' Didi looked up in amazement. 'Are you really suggesting that upon our arrival in Sanriol somebody bugged my phone? And when I returned to Artopolis, knocked me down to retrieve it just in case our security department decided to run a scan after I got back?'

Sasha shrugged noncommittally. 'Stranger things have happened when much less money was at stake. I suppose you've been to the police to report aggravated robbery?'

Didi was aghast. 'It is the furthest thing from my mind. Why do you say it?'

Sasha awkwardly shifted from foot to foot. 'The phone was company property. And loss of property should be reported. It could be wise to keep the Chief in the loop, too. Just in case, you know.'

Didi stayed pensive for a moment, then shrugged decisively. 'I suppose you're right. Now, could you roll that chair over here, please. Sorry for having kept you standing. Did you have a chance to review the project description draft I've sent you?'

Sasha looked only too glad to change the subject and get down to business. 'Sure, Didi. The first thing I'd like to talk about is the budget. What the board has decided is actually 800 artopools as the target, which can go up to 1,000 artopools if it's justified.'

Didi furiously scribbled in the notepad. 'Right, so it's 800 plus 200 cost tolerance. I'll need to update the project description. And while I'm at it, I notice that I haven't added you to the list of stakeholders yet. My mistake; will fix it at once. Is there anything else?'

Sasha scanned notes, pencilling in some remarks. 'Now, regarding the benefits. You've captured them correctly. But the fact is, they don't all have the same level of importance for

Artophyle. For example, earning money from renting out the Halls of Harmony is certainly an expected benefit, but for this project, it's not as important as the others. We have a number of projects that have the specific objective of generating profit.

The primary objective of HAHAP, as you call it, is different. It's primarily a lighthouse project that will make Artophyle highly visible in the world market. So, if we have to make compromises, in this case revenue-generating benefits are of lower importance.'

Didi pondered the implications of what Sasha had said, chewing on a pencil. 'Hm, that's an interesting angle. Placing weights on benefits can help me run the project while on delegated authority. I don't want to need to ask the sponsor to make every decision for me. I'll prefer to escalate only the really important decisions. And benefit-weighting will definitely help to sort the wheat from the chaff.

'So, if a decision concerns a low-priority benefit, I'd take it myself. But if a top-weighted benefit is involved, I'd better pass the decision on to Anan. And I suppose it'll be the sponsor who'll decide on benefit-weighting.'

Sasha nodded. 'The final decision will rest with Anan, possibly after checking with Artophyle board members.'

Didi pressed on. 'But let's kick the ball into play. What's your own perception?'

Sasha appeared unsure. 'I don't know if we're supposed to offer our own views. Anyway, the way I see it, the key expected benefit of HAHAP will be to promote Artophyle. Out of ten points, that one would merit four. As engaging with the community could also give Artophyle a boost in visibility, it gets two points. Engaging with the mayor of Artopolis might also deserve two points as it's sort of in-kind payback for the co-funding of the project. Having a top-class venue for our own events and obtaining revenue from commercial leases gets one point each.'

Sasha's phone chimed a reminder. 'Sorry Didi, I need to hurry now so as not to be late for another scheduled meeting. Was there anything else on your mind?'

Didi did a quick mental check. 'Actually, no, we've covered all the topics I've flagged. My apologies for trying to squeeze so many things into one discussion slot. But project initiation can occasionally get hectic.'

Didi quickly updated the project description.

Project Description V0.2 (draft)

Project name: Halls of Harmony (HAHAP)

Benefits:

- 4 - Promoting Artophyle Inc.
- 2 - Engaging w/the mayor of Artopolis
- 2 - Engaging with the community
- 1 - Having a venue for own events
- 1 - Obtaining revenue from leases

Cost and duration: 800 artopools and 24 months.

Tolerances: Cost tolerance 200 artopools.

Project product requirements and quality expectations: to be defined.

Stakeholders:

- Anan: sponsor, director of the S&M department
- Didi: project manager

- Sasha: project team member, S&M department
- Schwartz: Chairman of the Board of ArtoHolding
- Rilke: CEO
- Imani: director of the design department

The morning yielded only mediocre progress in the preparation of project description. Didi opted to skip lunch to catch up with the lag. Nothing unusual, really, and hence the importance of having a square meal in the morning. The morning fish soup still warmed the heart. Didi poured a mug of coffee and fetched a sesame seed and dried fruit bar from the vending machine. Not exactly health food, but Didi had no trouble stretching the definitions until they became fit for purpose.

While drinking coffee and munching on the bar, Didi streamed music through wireless in-ear phones. Completely disconnecting from the office reality for even fifteen minutes did marvels for concentration. A project manager had to make do with what they had.

Returning to the desk, Didi pulled thoughts together and decided to call the sponsor, with chowtime being the best time to get the executive's undivided attention. They hated such intrusions on their privacy and digestion but answered the ringing anyway. But Didi had no mobile phone. Not anymore. What a nuisance.

Under the circumstances, Didi came to appreciate the fact that the lounge area had a landline phone with a printout of department extensions taped to the table underneath it. 'Good afternoon, Anan, it's Didi speaking. Would you have a minute for a brief discussion?'

Anan sounded resigned. 'Oh, Didi, I should have known there'll be no respite from you. Next time, I'll have to treat you to lunch in order not to miss mine. What is it?'

Didi smiled; the trick had worked. 'Sorry, Anan, but that's the sponsor's cross. It'll get better after we've sailed through the Scylla and Charybdis of the project initiation. That is, unless you decide to micromanage me. Anyway, today's issue is that the project team is still missing a rep from Imani's shop. Could you gently squeeze the design department?'

Resignation in Anan's voice rose to irritation. 'I've talked to Imani about getting an architect for the project. Imani insisted that whenever you have an architectural task, you can send it up, and Imani will assign it for follow-up to someone in the department. Isn't that good enough for you?'

Didi counted till five before answering. 'I'm afraid not. It'll only mean that project tasks will be the lowest priority and, accordingly, our schedule slipping all the time. Project management is not same as business as usual. I insist on an appointment that will establish a direct line of subordination to me. Do I need to call Rilke regarding it?'

Didi realised that was a dangerous move. It implied readiness for mutiny. And what chief would tolerate it? But a kick in the ego might make the sponsor stop stalling on decision-taking.

Anan could barely stop irritation turning into ire. 'You've got a short fuse, Didi. Wouldn't double subordination create a complication?'

In for a penny, in for a pound. Didi opted for rubbing it in. 'No, if it's handled well. And I know how to handle it well. You can trust me. I've got experience.'

Anan trusted only intuition. Clearly, no benefit would accrue from starting an argument. 'You'll hear from me.'

About ten minutes later, Didi's scheduling app on the notebook pinged with a slot being taken. Azar from the design department had booked a meeting slot in an hour's time. When the company wheels got into motion, they moved fast.

Didi dialled the extension while perusing the lounge phone. 'Hi Azar, welcome aboard! I'm really glad to have you join the HAHAP team. I'll email you a copy of the draft project description next. Please have a look before we meet. Above all, I need more information about the requirements and quality expectations. Could you check with Imani to make sure it covers all bases for the purposes of high-level planning, please.'

Azar gave off a delighted laugh. 'Didi, your reputation precedes you. I'm really happy to be part of the HAHAP team. As you know, Imani only rarely agrees to appoint us to projects. Personally, I absolutely prefer it this way. I'll see you in the lounge on your floor.'

While waiting for Azar, Didi wrote a brief message to the Chief.

> Chief, today at around 8:40 in the morning, an unknown e-scooter rider knocked me down on the Artophyle plaza when I was finalising the arrangements for a HAHAP-related activity. As a consequence, I lost the grip on my mobile phone, which the rider scooped before disappearing. I deeply regret the loss of company property. Please advise in case I need to

> report the incident to the police. Hope that all is well at your end, Didi

Given the difference in the time zones and the Chief's primary duty to never leave the boss's side, the answer came back unexpectedly quickly. In Didi's view, such a banal issue didn't deserve this level of executive attention.

> Hey, Didi, sorry to hear that. I do think it may be a good idea to file a police report. But do not refer to it in office conversations, generally downplaying the gravity of the incident. Stay on the alert, I can't exclude the possibility of your becoming the target of further hostile activity. Do not, repeat, do not as much as mention your being aware of the project we are progressing here. I've raised a requisition with property control so that you may get a new phone. Keep safe, Chief

Didi could only shake the head in utter bewilderment, clueless about the reasons for Chief's concerns.

Azar dropped into the chair in front. 'Afternoon, Didi. You know, Imani got positively mad when I had barged into the office yelling, "Urgent business, urgent business, I'm on a mission from Didi".'

Didi's eyes widened. 'Shoot, you didn't do that Azar…or you did?!'

Azar laughed like crazy, jumping in the chair and beating the armrests with both hands. 'Got you Didi, got you! Yeah, I wish I did it. Maybe next time. I'm sure working on this project will offer me plenty of opportunities.

'Now, regarding product requirements and quality expectations. When we submitted the bid for that invitation to tender, it included a detailed specifications folder. That is typically the first delivery step in a construction project. And a delivery step is a sequence or set of work packages aimed to produce an interim output, in this case, our specifications brochure.

'By the way, the lead on this bid is with Noor, the most senior architect in Artophyle. No important design decision is made without Noor on board.'

Didi got the drift at once. 'Since Noor is certain to have a weighty opinion on every project aspect, let me update the list of stakeholders right away then.'

Azar nodded in appreciation before continuing. 'The most general requirement you can deduce yourself. The Halls of Harmony should be suitable for hosting the Save the Planet Award ceremony. That stretched our typical capacity vision far beyond its usual boundaries.

'In the past, we had thought that aiming for some 400 event attendees was a tad brave, and planning for 600 would be adventurous but still borderline rational.'

Didi picked up after the full stop. 'But the Save the Planet Award ceremony will require a more capacious venue.'

Azar made a happy grimace, accompanied by the palms-up gesture. 'You are spot on. And we suddenly reckoned, one reason why really large events hadn't been held in Artopolis was because there weren't many venues that could support them. So, after chewing on the bone for a while, Imani approved going for a design that would hold 5000 attendees, and also include a huge backstage area and a separate storage for furniture and trappings.'

Didi remained aloof, not quite sharing Azar's enthusiasm. 'But that's going out on a limb. If it stands idle, the maintenance cost will sink Artophyle!'

Azar winked at Didi, raising an index finger in the air for emphasis. 'Naturally, there's a business case for that. Our design specification also provides for all possible kinds of business events, as well as artistic and cultural ones, too, like art exhibitions, gala award ceremonies, rock group concerts, motocross races, party caucuses and anything that would fit in between.

'But those dazzling heights and dizzying operational and marketing challenges shouldn't rob you, my friend, of your well-deserved night's sleep or project manager's zeal. HAHAP's objective is to build the Halls of Harmony, not to run it. There are greater minds who focus on strategic issues like the business case and are capable of making the necessary leap of faith.'

Didi shrugged and nodded. It made perfect sense to stay rooted in the project manager's responsibilities. The business case would be drawn up and realised at the higher level of authority. 'Point taken. What comes next?'

Azar picked up the thread without breaking stride. 'Next comes the interior. In the beginning, we thought of having fancy décor with all possible trappings, a luxurious setting. But then we realised that it might be grossly out of place for, say, a motocross event. So, in the end, we decided to keep it as minimalistic as P3.express.' Azar winked again, grinning from ear to ear, 'Many events will create their own atmosphere. And that is only possible with a bare-bones interior. Incidentally, it will help lower the costs a bit.'

Didi nodded again, this time pensively. 'And a simple interior will also endure while changes in vogue might make a fancy design obsolete in as little as a few years' time.

'But what about the exterior design?'

Now it was Azar's time to nod, radiating unreserved enthusiasm. 'We aim to create a landmark for Artopolis with a design of exceptional beauty. After all, we are an architectural firm! That design will incorporate abundant attributes of climate-protecting technologies, like overall climate neutrality, reduced energy consumption, solar panels for hot water, photovoltaic panels for electricity generation and maybe even a small wind farm.'

Didi summed it up. 'Right, Azar, thanks for your help. If my notes are correct, there are nine core requirements and connected quality expectations:

1. Capacity for 5000 attendees/spectators.
2. Multi-functionality.
3. Huge backstage area.
4. Large storage area.
5. Minimalist interior design that can be adapted to different types of events.
6. Landmark exterior design.
7. Overall climate neutrality.
8. Solar panels for water heating.
9. Photovoltaic panels for electricity generation.

'I'd prefer to leave the wind farm out for the time being; we can always add it to the project description at a later stage. After all, a project description is a living document. We'll review and revise it regularly during project delivery.'

Azar looked delighted. 'That's smoking!'

Didi baselined the project description, adding new information.

Project Description V0.3 (draft).

Project name: Halls of Harmony (HAHAP)

Benefits:

▓▓▓▓▓▓▓▓▓▓▓ ██ 4 - Promoting Artophyle Inc.

▓▓▓▓▓▓▓▓▓▓▓▓▓ █ 2 - Engaging with the Mayor of Artopolis

▓▓▓▓▓▓▓▓▓▓▓▓▓ █ 2 - Engaging with the community

▓▓▓▓▓▓▓▓▓▓▓▓▓▓▓ █ 1 - Having a venue for own events

▓▓▓▓▓▓▓▓▓▓▓▓▓▓ █ 1 - Obtaining revenue from leases

Cost and duration: 800 artopools and 24 months.

Tolerances: Cost tolerance 200 artopools.

Project product requirements and quality expectations:

- Capacity for 5000 attendees/spectators.
- Multi-functionality.
- Huge backstage area.
- Large storage area.
- Minimalist interior design that can be adapted to different types of events.
- Landmark exterior design.
- Overall climate neutrality.
- Water heating with solar panels.
- Electricity generation with photovoltaic panels.

Stakeholders:

- Anan: sponsor, director of the S&M department
- Didi: project manager

- Sasha: project team member, S&M department staff
- Azar: project team member, design department staff
- Schwartz: Chairman of the Board of ArtoHolding
- Rilke: CEO
- Imani: director of the design department
- Noor: senior architect, design lead

* * *

Outside, it was dark already. The rush of work had ebbed and Didi felt tiredness sweep over like a wave. The catch of the day was the updated version of the project description. Didi decided to show true grit and finish the job.

Before starting work on Activity 05 – Identify and plan the deliverables it made good sense to completely close Activity 04 related to the project description first. Running management activities in parallel or with overlaps was fraught with the risk of doing everything at once and achieving nothing.

Being a fundamental, strategic document, the project description required formal sponsor approval. Earlier in the day, Didi had been tempted to ask Sasha to take it up with Anan. After all, they worked in the same department. If Anan found any issues, Sasha would then provide feedback.

But what if Sasha didn't clearly explain to Anan the purpose of the review and the importance of sponsor's approval? Or if Sasha didn't draw Anan's attention to the advisability of bringing it to the attention of other board members?

While the HAHAP project description needed to be aligned with Artophyle's portfolio business case, it remained unclear whether Anan clearly understood this requirement.

Conclusion: suit the action to the words. Or as it might be, thoughts.

> Anan,
>
> The HAHAP project team have agreed on the initial version of the project description (see attached). Imani's and your own opinion have been sought on its specific elements. This time, kindly review the whole document and indicate your approval if you have no objections. Please note that I leave it to you to decide whether there's anyone higher up in the organisation whose opinion or other input you consider opportune to seek. Individual project descriptions need to conform to the Artophyle's portfolio business case.
>
> Looking forward to receiving your reply,
>
> Didi

Having sent the email, Didi sat back to think what else needed to be done and almost immediately, decided to draft a short message to the other two project team members.

> Sasha and Azar, thanks a lot for your highly valued inputs. The first version of the Project Description has been sent for the project sponsor's approval. I attach it for your perusal and to ensure that all of us are singing from the same page. As we proceed with project delivery, we'll review and update the project description as may become necessary and seek new approval. Regards, Didi

A ping announcing the arrival of an elevator cabin resonated in the empty floor. Didi heard someone storm onto the floor. 'Ah, there you are' Anan's voice carried through space. 'Why the dickens are you not answering your phone?'

Didi waited until Anan came closer before answering. 'Because somebody knocked me down in the morning and stole it.'

For a moment Anan appeared at a loss over what to say, calming down a bit in the process of searching for words. 'Right, I see, well, you don't look like you have been hurt or anything. Good. Now, look, Didi, it's still very early in the project and I can't approve the project description because a lot of things remain unclear or may change. Let's first iron all the creases out, OK?'

Didi sighed, at least mentally. 'I'm so used to it. Whenever I ask someone to approve something, the first reaction is panicky rejection'.

Out loud, Didi used the best soothing voice. 'Anan, your approval won't mean that the project description becomes set in stone. It just gives us confirmation that our current understanding of the project, as described in the project description, is correctly aligned with what the organisation has in mind.

We'll use this understanding to proceed with project initiation. Project description is a fluid document under version control. As we move through the project life cycle, it will require many reviews and adjustments. And I'll be asking for your approval time and again.'

'So, get used to it and stop acting like the Cowardly Lion' muttered Didi under the breath. And going back to full volume, completed the sponsor's education. 'All I need from you is to confirm that the project description is good enough for now. You may wish to check with other Artophyle executives as you feel necessary.'

Anan looked and sounded relieved. 'Now I understand what you're looking for. It's different from what I usually call approval as department director. Anyway, the document you've sent me seems fine. To be on the safe side, tomorrow I'll check with the other board members and to be on the safe side, send it for Rilke's attention, too. Whether it merits the boss's attention or not, that's another story, but at least I've laid it at the supremo's feet. I'll let you know as soon I get feedback.

'And in the meantime, fix yourself with a new phone. Do you need me to sign a requisition?'

Didi, mission on a firm track to success, was all smiles. 'Thank you, Anan, the Chief has already sent the authorisation to property control.'

Anan chuckled approvingly and winked in feigned awe. 'Oh, I see you've got friends in high places, Didi. You fly around in business jets and stay in government residences. Looks like you are becoming a figure on the corporate gameboard that one needs to reckon with.'

Didi made a face in return.

* * *

It was time to pay a visit to the police precinct, the last remaining item of the day's programme. It was getting late. The flow of traffic on Grand Concourse slowly ebbed. The hoodies at the stairs to the Metro had chosen another place to meet, and Didi somehow felt relieved by it.

The precinct building stood in a narrow side street only a few blocks away in the direction of Place Etoile, and Didi decided to walk. After a full day spent mostly sitting stooped over the desk, it felt like a release to stretch the legs and start the blood pumping.

In the warmer months, the broad pedestrian boulevard flanking the Grand Concourse with a row of open-air cafés and lounges flourished as a round-the-clock flaneurs' paradise. This time of the year though, it remained mostly empty of human traffic, despite the inviting weather filled with the first faint fragrances of the budding spring.

At first, Didi hobbled along clenching teeth against the pain. The injuries from the attack were taking effect. After a while, though, the going got easier. The blood flow started restoring the hurt tissue and the pain abated. That was a feature of Didi's character: whenever knocked down, stand up and move on.

The precinct building looked older than dirt and a bit derelict on the outside, its unpainted walls of red brick rising to the steeply angled roof pecked by time and the shrapnel of ancient wars. Arm-thick bars on thumbnail windows gave it the overall appearance of a medieval prison, which in all probability was at least partly intentional.

The day shift was coming to an end, and the handover occurred at an unhurried pace. The incoming cops looked cool and composed compared with their tense and dishevelled-looking outgoing colleagues. Didi had to wait for half an hour sitting on a plastic bench bolted to the hard-scrubbed vinyl floor that reeked of antiseptic, with a water cooler the only amenity for visitors.

At long last, the duty officer behind an armoured glass partition motioned Didi to come forward. A tablet securely attached to the narrow counter running the length of the partition came to life. Didi scanned the personal ID and filled in the fields of an incident report. The duty officer checked and nodded, waiving Didi goodbye.

Back on the boulevard, Didi considered the options. It was going on midnight. A ride in a rickshaw presented easily the most tempting one, but they never cruised the streets at this late hour. And Didi had no phone to call one. And, besides, the Metro would still run for two hours, with the nearest station only a block or so away.

Despite the late hour, the train to Place Etoile arrived predictably full, though not packed. The Central line traversed the corporate and entertainment districts, both still busy at that time of night. And at the Etoile station, platforms and walkways at its different levels thronged with people at all angles of the clock. Artopolis's five Metro lines and the cable-car line to the airport converged there.

It was close to half past midnight. As intervals between Southern line trains became pretty long at that hour, Didi had to wait for about thirty minutes. Suddenly becoming alert and apprehensive for no apparent reason, Didi scanned the deserted platform with its scattering of riders. Nothing seemed out of the normal. But then out of the corner of an eye, Didi caught movement at the station stairs. A figure in a hoodie with the hood pulled up descended the steps and slowly but purposefully strolled down the platform in Didi's general direction.

For some baffling reason, Didi's heart sank. It all seemed so weird. The train arrived and Didi hopped on it with relief, taking one of the many empty seats. A newer model, the train had the articulated design with a doorless passage connecting the carriages. Riding in the first coach, Didi could observe the whole 100-metre long train tube bending this way and that as it barrelled along the curvy track.

When the train twisted left to right, Didi had a moment's glimpse of the full length of the central passage, including a hooded figure walking up the train. When the carriages briefly realigned in a straight line, the figure came nearer. Another bend of the tracks, and the train entered a station. Didi had a panicky urge to alight on the platform and run.

The whole situation felt ridiculous. How could a lone Metro rider of a harmless appearance strike such terror in Didi's heart? It was unbelievable and because of that, even scarier. The train left the lights of the station behind and re-entered the pitch-dark tunnel. A moment later, the hooded figure entered Didi's carriage and halted, grabbing with both hands the support bars running on the sides of the aisle.

The train lurched and rocked. The figure stood still as if scanning the carriage. Then the figure moved on, at a slow pace, finally choosing to take a seat right in front of Didi in the all but empty carriage.

As suddenly as Didi's fear had come, it lifted, leaving curiosity in its wake. What the deuce was going on? The figure sat in a poised posture with head slightly lowered so that the face remained concealed by the hood. And that was how they travelled the remaining stretch of the line.

At Loranca station, Didi alighted from the train and went up the stairs to the street without casting a single glance back. On a few occasions Didi felt fellow riders briefly brushing against the peacoat but never paid it any attention. On packed trains and in crowded stations, body contact occurred all the time. Didi's fear had given to curiosity, and curiosity, to indifference.

Most of the food stalls had closed for the night, but a few always stayed open to serve the night owls. Despite going through the day on a single granola bar and a gallon of watery filter coffee, Didi felt no hunger. A pair of tamales would keep the coals glowing until the time of the morning soup.

During the red-eye hours, tuctucs ran on demand. Once ten out of twelve passenger seats were filled, the driver shot off into the night streets that otherwise stayed empty of soul or engine. The ride across the mostly asleep South-of-the-river took a wink of an eye. At the apartment door, Didi patted at pockets for keys and found them in the company of the misappropriated mobile phone. It was going on two in the morning.

At the precinct, the nightshift detective who went by the name of Klebb looked pensively at the results of the query on the police database. When filed and stored, Didi's incident report had triggered a complicated search algorithm that raised a flag. And for the better part of the last four hours, Klebb tried to figure out what went on on their turf. And it looked like something did.

Video footage of the assault on Didi, captured by one of the ubiquitous cameras, hadn't revealed much. That is, until it went to the analytic unit of the Artopolis police department. The nimble catch of Didi's phone turned out to be a signature movement of a known criminal operator, currently sought for several daring assaults. The skilled and enterprising perpetrator served as a hired gun or in this instance, hand. It robbed the whole incident of its seeming spontaneity, transforming it into a premeditated and meticulously planned and executed contract hit. This conclusion didn't raise Klebb's spirits.

* * *

Didi slept fitfully and woke feeling tired from the roller coaster ride provided by the day before. The bruises displayed a mood-raising variety of hues ranging from infant poo to luscious violet. As walking still hurt and there was little chance of remaining glued to a tuctuc side board, Didi surrendered to the obvious and flagged a cruising rickshaw.

A thick and fragrantly spiced red lentil and bulgur soup at the Loranca station stalls provided the indispensable kick-start to the day. While crossing the small plaza before the Artophyle tower, Didi remained on full alert, scanning the surroundings for villainous e-rollers and iniquitous hoody-wearers, observing neither.

A05 - Identify and plan the deliverables

HAVING ACHIEVED the brilliant success of making it to the office all in one piece, Didi could concentrate on the day's schedule. The core task was Activity A05 – Identify and plan the deliverables leading to the creation of a deliverables map. Its preparation required the participation of subject experts from more Artophyle departments.

In Didi's experience, conducting a workshop invariably served as the most result-orientated and time-efficient way of putting together a deliverables map. It could be relied on to provide induction through immersion to newly-appointed project team members and offer an excellent team-building opportunity, too.

But first, departments had to be persuaded, convinced or coerced into appointing their experts to the HAHAP team. That was no mean feat that required the use of strong managerial muscle. Didi called Anan but got the director's assistant instead. 'Hey Didi. Anan is tied up in a meeting, I'm afraid. It may continue until dark. Maybe I could help you in the meantime?'

Didi hesitated for a moment. As the issue at hand involved diplomatic persuasion further enhanced by a bit of arm-twisting, rather than decision-taking, it seemed worth it to play the odds. 'Right, thank you. Could you then call the directors of the mechanical engineering and electrical engineering departments, Eka and Darci, and on Anan's authority ask them to appoint their department experts to the HAHAP team, please. And, kind of, now?'

The voice of Anan's assistant carried a note of hesitation. 'But Anan hasn't taken the go/no-go decision yet. So, the project has not been formally approved. Department directors may say it as an excuse for an objection.'

Didi didn't miss a beat. 'Anan has approved project initiation and the specialists from different departments will precisely work to prepare the documentation for an informed go/no-go decision by the sponsor. Rilke has appointed the project sponsor and the rest is now up to Anan.'

The assistant made some quick reckoning and acquiesced. 'Oh, sure, now I understand. No worries; I've run more delicate errands for Anan.'

Not quite believing the good luck, Didi went several floors up to property controls to pick up a replacement phone. It was in mint condition but otherwise identical to its battle-scarred predecessor. That took all of five minutes. It seemed only prudent to not complicate things any further by admitting that the stolen phone had somehow found its way back to its owner's peacoat pocket.

This last circumstance made Didi wonder. Why had the goons gone through all the trouble involved in returning the phone? Maybe to encourage Didi to withdraw the incident report? No report, no investigation. Did the thugs have a reason to fear discovery?

The new phone woke up to duty with gusto, pinging with text messages that had accumulated during the past forty-eight hours.

> Hey Didi, it's Monet from the electrical engineering department. What a pleasant surprise! Looking forward to joining your team. Let me know how I could be of help.

> Morning Didi, my name's Kim and I work in the mechanical engineering department. My director Eka has just told me that I should report for duty with the project team. I'm not quite familiar with what it means, so I'd appreciate getting to learn the ropes. Please be aware that the amount of time I can contribute to HAHAP is limited because our department has a deadline for a major delivery in three weeks' time that is labelled our departmental priority. Eka let me join the team grinding the teeth.

That sounded as good as it got and Didi lost not a minute in launching an assault on the notebook's keyboard.

> Dear project team members,
> We're initiating the Halls of Harmony project, or HAHAP in short, and at this point, I need your help with preparing the deliverables map.

While the project description that was finalised yesterday and is now pending the sponsor's approval has a focus on the requirements and quality expectations regarding the project's final product, the deliverables map aims to decompose the final output into its constituent configuration items and create their hierarchical breakdown.

Our starting point will be the project description, an updated version of which you can find below. Please take a look at it before the meeting.

Project Description V0.4 (draft).

Project name: Halls of Harmony (HAHAP)

Benefits:

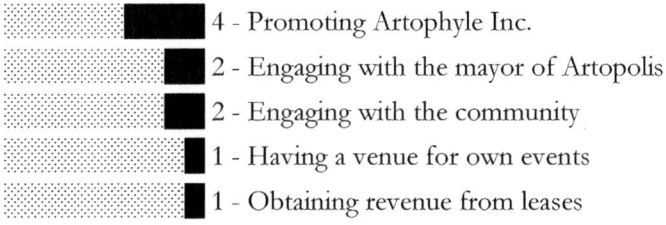

4 - Promoting Artophyle Inc.
2 - Engaging with the mayor of Artopolis
2 - Engaging with the community
1 - Having a venue for own events
1 - Obtaining revenue from leases

Cost and duration: 800 artopools and 24 months.

Tolerances: Cost tolerance 200 artopools.

Project product requirements and quality expectations:

- Capacity for 5000 attendees/spectators.
- Multi-functionality.
- Huge backstage area.
- Large storage area.
- Minimalist interior design that can be adapted to different types of events.
- Landmark exterior design.
- Overall climate neutrality.

- Water heating with solar panels.
- Electricity generation with photovoltaic panels.

Stakeholders:

- Anan: sponsor, director of the S&M Department
- Didi: project manager
- Sasha: project team member, S&M Department staff
- Azar: project team member, Design Department staff
- Monet: project team member, Electrical Engineering Department staff
- Kim: project team member, Mechanical Engineering Department staff
- Schwartz: Chairman of the Board of ArtoHolding
- Rilke: CEO
- Imani: director of the Design department
- Noor: senior architect, design lead
- Eka: director of the Mechanical Engineering Department
- Darci: director of the Electrical Engineering Department.

Let's get together for an hour or so during lunchtime and have a meet & eat workshop. Since this will be our first one, please bring your own food so that I could find out about your tastes and preferences.

Looking forward to seeing you all soon,

Didi

In an effort to help the workshop participants avoid being affected by 'blank page syndrome' that at a very minimum, led to loss of time, Didi decided to sketch the main elements of the future deliverables map.

> **Main building**
> Main Hall of Harmony
> > TV commentators' booths
> > Configuration and transformation machinery
>
> Hall of Harmony#2
> > Meeting room 2.1
> > WC#1
> > Meeting room 2.2
> > WC#2
> > Kitchen#1
> > Simultaneous interpretation booths
> > WC#3
>
> Hall of Harmony#3
> > Meeting room 3.1
> > Meeting room 3.2
> > Meeting room 3.3
> > Kitchen#2
>
> Rotunda (central vestibule)
> Backstage section
> **Storage building**
> **Surroundings**
> **Site preparation** (demolition of the old warehouse).

The project thus would include four major deliverables – site preparation, main building, storage building and surroundings although it went without saying that they didn't all have the same importance to the project and level of technical complexity. To Didi, that looked good enough to kick-start the workshop and release the flow of technical comments.

When the Artophyle tower started emptying around noon, discharging a steady flow of lunch-eaters, Sasha, Azar, Monet and Kim joined Didi in the floor lounge for the meet and eat. Sasha brought some chicken kebab with yoghurt and cucumber dip. Azar's fare included a roasted aubergine wrap with a side of ḥummuṣ bi ṭaḥini. Monet went for a serving of home-cooked lasagne. Kim choose a box of rice cakes and fish cakes in chilli paste.

Clutching the mundane granola bar, Didi felt like a caveman. 'Right, pals, let me kick off while you are munching. Our next objective is to produce a deliverables map. As it reflects the hierarchy of configuration items, we'll aim to include dependencies between them, adding where useful explanations regarding their scope and quality expectations.

'The deliverables map will provide us with the backbone for scheduling. When there are many dependencies, we can schedule the elements on the basis of their dependencies and estimated durations. When, on the other hand, dependencies are comparatively few, we can prioritise the elements in accordance with an agreed set of criteria. In this case, the sequence of their execution will base on priorities and improvisation rather than a schedule.

'In real life these polar conceptual approaches can be combined. The higher levels of planning use a dependency-based method and the lower levels, a priority-based technique. In our case, however, the latter would hardly work as, due to its nature, construction follows the predictive approach.

'Let's start with design. Azar, the floor is yours.'

Azar nodded enthusiastically. 'As with most of Noor's designs, the Halls of Harmony symbolise the umbilical cord between people and nature. We all are children of nature and should never forget to revere and respect the womb, from which we came.

'This reflection explains the emphasis on the use of solar panels and wind turbines. But more importantly, Noor's design radiates a statement against wilful destruction of nature, together with the belief in its phoenix powers. It resembles stumps of cut trees from which new saplings are springing up.

'As you can see, most of the site will be covered in gardens and a medium-sized natural forest that will hide from sight the parking lots and driveways or walkways. As a consequence, all of these three elements of the surroundings will require quite a bit of earthwork. Instead of paving, surfaces will be covered in flagstones that allow rain drainage and let the soil breathe. On top of that, the gardens will require a heavy bit of landscaping, plus watering and the plants proper, of course.'

Didi was busy working the mind-mapping app. 'Should I assume, there may be a few structural or civil engineering elements that have been omitted from the tender package?'

Azar sounded apologetic. 'The design specifications are only the tip of the iceberg. There are also hook-ups to the municipal water supply and sewage disposal systems, flood drains, as well as some other stuff. But all of that will be accounted for during the designing delivery step. It will produce the detailed blueprints for each component of the project and help us to improve on the granularity of the deliverables map and its utility for scheduling the monthly work cycles.

'Take temporary structures, for example. On site, we'll put up a whole small town of Conex buildings made up of customisable and stackable containers to provide changing rooms and ablution facilities for the army of construction workers, kitchen, eating rooms, a small infirmary with sickbay for medical emergencies and so on.

'They will sure be temporary but will still need to be set up, which qualifies them as deliverables.'

Didi finally got an opportunity to bite into the granola bar. In hindsight, opting for a snack had been a wise choice for the note-taker. 'Thank you, Azar. I guess that should be sufficient for now. The deliverables map, like every other management control in P3.express, is prepared following the incremental approach. It doesn't need to be perfectly complete right from the start.

'Kim, you're next.'

Having long since polished off the small box of food and being halfway through a cup of coffee, Kim's high spirits reached full blaze, radiating benevolence and generosity. 'For a start, we'll need deliverables relating to site mobilisation, demolition of the old warehouse and site clearing. We'll work on what's called a brownfield site and it'll be more time- and resource-consuming to mobilise and run.

'Next comes pit preparation and pouring the building foundations. You can present it either as a single deliverable for the whole facility or as lower-level deliverables for each of the building elements, like Main Hall, Hall of Harmony #2,

Hall of Harmony #3, storage building and so on. Mind you, individual foundations are no small thing and presenting them as deliverables under separate building elements headers will be fully justified.

'Then, each of the building elements will include a set of construction components including walls, windows, doors, ceiling, floor, and so on. Doors and windows may be reflected as subsets of walls.

'The walls themselves will be load-bearing concrete with built-in insulation and colour that will be left exposed on both the outside and the inside. That means we won't have separate elements for insulation, painting, and the like. We'll only need to have acoustic treatment on the inside.'

Didi raised a hand. 'Kim, thank you for your methodical approach, but could I suggest we stop here for the time being. There is more than sufficient information for initial scheduling and we'll delve deeper during monthly initiation.

'Monet, it's your turn now.'

Monet looked a bit fidgety. 'Hey, Didi, I'm afraid we're running a bit late going through all this tremendous amount of detail. I know it's important, but I suggest that now in project initiation you pull the plug somewhere. Much of what we are discussing will become truly relevant only during monthly initiation. And between now and then, a lot of water will pass under the bridge.

'If you allow, I'll focus just on the essentials.

'For a start, we need to install a photovoltaic array to provide the juice and run electrical cabling and wiring to power lighting, a computer network, and an audio system for simultaneous interpretation, speeches, music and public address, as well as fire sensors and sprinklers. Another deliverable would be the industrial-current cable tree to power the air conditioning and heating. By the way, heating, ventilation and air conditioning is usually abbreviated to HVAC.

'As you see, electrical deliverables connect to a whole group of mechanical ones and I'll work closely with Kim to agree who'll take the lead on each one. My gut feeling says that most are more of a mechanical nature and for such my department will serve in the supplier's role.

From my perspective, cabling for a particular hall will form part of the higher-level cabling deliverable. But if you prefer, you can treat, say, cabling for the Hall of Harmony #2 as an element of that deliverable. Since at this moment I can't say, which approach will result in a smoother project delivery, it's your call, and we can always regroup on the fly.

'Though in any case, I suggest not to go as far as including electrical installations as components of deliverables like floor, ceiling or walls.'

Didi's fingers on the keypad were smoking with inserting all this detail into the deliverables map that was expanding like rising dough. Now Didi paused, chewing on the lower lip. 'I can think of two ways to resolve this dilemma. One option is to rename the existing floor, walls, and ceiling items into something that makes it clear that they only contain the structure and finish. And the second option is to add another layer: one for the structure and finish, one for the mechanical, electrical, and piping items.'

Monet frowned. 'Adding another layer will make the map too crowded. I like the first option better.'

Didi resumed working the keyboard and the mouse. 'Right-o. Consider it done. And I suggest we stop here. A construction project inevitably produces a fiendishly complex deliverables map. But it's starting to take shape. We'll leave it as a high-level overview at this stage and then dig deeper for specific deliverables during monthly initiations. Thank you for your time!'

Alone in the floor lounge, Didi lustily dug into the stub of the granola bar, washing it down with cold coffee. It was getting a bit late for this spartan lunch, even by Didi's elastic standards. But better late than never!

To put on record the most recent accomplishment of the project team, Didi fired off a summary email to the team members.

> Dear colleagues,
>
> attached is the initial HAHAP deliverables map. Please note that it is what it is called – a hierarchically organised map that reflects the conceptual order of deliverables – and not a schedule reflecting the order of execution. In short, it's about "what" rather than "when". This is the team's internal working document that does not require any higher approvals. You're already familiar with it as it's based on your contributions, but having the final copy may be helpful. We will refine and revise it throughout the project, at the very least during monthly initiations, and use as the basis for scheduling monthly work cycles. However, whenever you see the need for making an

> adjustment or find an issue with it, please let me know immediately so that we can quickly agree on corrective action.
>
> Regards,
>
> Didi

Deliverables map V.1.0 (project initiation)

1. Site mobilisation
2. Conex container camp set up and operational
3. Demolition of the warehouse
4. Site clearing
5. Pit prepared and foundation poured
6. Main building
    6.1. Administration offices
    6.2. IT room
    6.3. Security room
    6.4. UHF communication network
    6.5. Grand Hall of Harmony
        6.5.1. Floor structure & finish
        6.5.2. Walls structure & finish
        6.5.3. Ceiling structure & finish
        6.5.4. Lighting
        6.5.5. Computer network
        6.5.6. Music/PA system
        6.5.7. HVAC
        6.5.8. Fire protection
        6.5.9. Furniture
        6.5.10. TV commentators' booths
        6.5.11. Configuration and transformation machinery
    6.6. Hall of Harmony#2
        6.6.1. Floor structure & finish
        6.6.2. Walls structure & finish
        6.6.3. Ceiling structure & finish
        6.6.4. Lighting
        6.6.5. Computer network
        6.6.6. Music/PA system
        6.6.7. HVAC
        6.6.8. Fire protection

6.6.9. Furniture
6.6.10. Meeting room 2.1
- 6.6.10.1. Walls structure & finish
- 6.6.10.2. Computer network
- 6.6.10.3. Music/PA system
- 6.6.10.4. HVAC
- 6.6.10.5. Furniture
- 6.6.10.6. WC#1
    - 6.6.10.6.1. Floor structure & finish
    - 6.6.10.6.2. Walls structure & finish
    - 6.6.10.6.3. Ceiling structure & finish
    - 6.6.10.6.4. Lighting
    - 6.6.10.6.5. Music/PA system
    - 6.6.10.6.6. HVAC
    - 6.6.10.6.7. Fire protection
    - 6.6.10.6.8. Sanitary appliances and equipment

6.6.11. Meeting room 2.2
- 6.6.11.1. Walls structure & finish
- 6.6.11.2. Computer network
- 6.6.11.3. Music/PA system
- 6.6.11.4. HVAC
- 6.6.11.5. Furniture
- 6.6.11.6. WC#2
    - 6.6.11.6.1. Floor structure & finish
    - 6.6.11.6.2. Walls structure & finish
    - 6.6.11.6.3. Ceiling structure & finish
    - 6.6.11.6.4. Lighting
    - 6.6.11.6.5. Music/PA system
    - 6.6.11.6.6. HVAC
    - 6.6.11.6.7. Fire protection
    - 6.6.11.6.8. Sanitary appliances and equipment
- 6.6.11.7. Kitchen
    - 6.6.11.7.1. Kitchen appliances and equipment
- 6.6.11.8. Simultaneous interpretation booths

6.7. Hall of Harmony#3
- 6.7.1. Floor structure & finish
- 6.7.2. Walls structure & finish
- 6.7.3. Ceiling structure & finish
- 6.7.4. Lighting
- 6.7.5. Computer network

       6.7.6. Music/PA system
       6.7.7. HVAC
       6.7.8. Fire protection
       6.7.9. Furniture
           6.7.9.1. Meeting room 3.1
           6.7.9.2. Meeting room 3.2
           6.7.9.3. Meeting room 3.3
7. Rotunda (central vestibule with foyer)
8. Backstage section
9. Storage building
   9.1. Floor structure & finish
   9.2. Walls structure & finish
   9.3. Ceiling structure & finish
10. Surroundings
   10.1. Parking lot with driveways
       10.1.1. Earthwork
       10.1.2. Stonework
       10.1.3. Paving
       10.1.4. Lighting
       10.1.5. Signage
   10.2. Gardens
       10.2.1. Landscaping
       10.2.2. Walkways
       10.2.3. Lighting
       10.2.4. Watering
       10.2.5. Plants
   10.3. Woods
       10.3.1. Landscaping
       10.3.2. Trees
       10.3.3. Shrubs
       10.3.4. Birds

The sponsor's formal approval of the deliverables map was not required. Still, organisational courtesy and common sense suggested that Anan be informed about the completion of milestone activities.

> Hello Anan, we're done preparing the initial deliverables map of the project. This is the project team's internal working

> document that does not require your formal approval. Still, to keep you in the loop, I attach it for your information. Regards, Didi

The next task of Activity A05 focused on scheduling. As if on cue, Didi's phone pinged with an incoming message.

> Come and see me right away. Anan

Didi pondered this new development for a moment. Did it spell trouble? The curtness of the sponsor's message was no indicator of the executive's mood; Anan preferred to save on verbal frills and stick to the subject.

Anan's lair occupied a suite of offices several floors up and entering it felt like passing from budget economy into first. There was wood panelling, frosted glass, genuine leather, paintings on the wall and finely chosen colour cadences. Artophyle's image emphasised class and quality. Anan's assistant buzzed the boss on the intercom. 'Didi is here to see you.'

Didi entered the sanctum. Anan towered behind the monumental desk, put together like a Victorian bridge. At its conference extension sat a new face, looking fresh from the mint. Anan waved Didi to take a seat next to the fresh cannon fodder and cut to the bone without preamble. 'We've got an infusion of new blood. Interns. Meet here Mirai, who's a master's student in project management, with a minor in scheduling. I think you can put this resource to good use. What's your take?'

As if Anan allowed Didi to have any diverging thoughts on the subject. 'Sure, Chief. Delighted to meet you, Mirai.'

Anan grunted. 'Then get to work, the two of you. The sun is still high in sky.'

This last statement seemed an exaggeration at half five in the afternoon, but Didi felt no inclination for picking an argument with Anan over such a trivial matter. Besides, the memory of internship stayed forever imprinted on Didi's mind.

In those times, getting an opportunity for on-the-job learning required serious scheming and plenty of luck. Few managers had displayed enthusiasm for accepting interns. Needless to say, such prevailing attitudes had made it very difficult for young professionals to get started in their careers. Still did, as a matter of fact.

Descending several flights of stairs to their floor, Didi couldn't help but get swept away by the train of memories. 'I remember my internship manager, Cruz. Very nice person. The first time I met Cruz, I said "Thanks for accepting me" and Cruz replied, "When I had been feverishly seeking internship opportunities, clutching at straws to give a push to my fledgling career, someone else had accepted me and taught me a lot. Now it's my turn to pay it forward".'

And so now Didi's turn came to send the elevator back and offer Mirai a ride up the career ladder. Time flew like in a dream. Didi sat down at the desk and asked Mirai to drag over a chair. 'All right, Mirai, here is your copy of the project description and the deliverables map. Take the necessary time to study them. Your task is to prepare a high-level schedule, in consultation with Azar, Kim and Monet.'

Mirai looked a bit disorientated by the snowballing of events but otherwise radiated happiness. 'Oh, Didi, first of all, thank you very much for accepting me as your intern. You can count on my doing the absolute best I can. I'm quite experienced in scheduling, albeit, you know, in simulations. We've gone through loads of case studies at the university.

'You only need to decide which type of scheduling is more appropriate in P3.express - a dependency-based technique like critical paths, or a priority-based one using a task board or a Kanban board?'

Didi smiled. 'You've asked the right question, Mirai. Either of the above techniques can be used in P3.express, depending on the project product. There are many dependencies in a construction project, and those provide the main criterion for deciding on the order of work packages. As a result, we'll use a dependency-based schedule.'

Mirai nodded, but with a hint of a doubt. 'Could I clarify something, Didi? You know, being an intern, I am disposed of an inquisitive mind. Don't all projects have dependencies of some sort?'

Didi felt impatience starting to stir but quashed it. 'You are spot on when you say, "of some sort". It's a matter of degree. To give you an example, in some IT projects, you can determine project deliverables in a way that minimises dependencies. In those circumstances, you'll be able to prioritise work package execution using a set of your own criteria. That's the case when you could use a priority-based schedule, like those you see on task boards or Kanban boards.'

This time Mirai's nodding was free from doubt. 'Got it. Makes sense to me. I'll prepare a dependency-based schedule. Should it be high-level or detailed?'

Didi couldn't help but be impressed with Mirai's tenacity and attention to detail. 'We are now in project initiation. The current requirement is to create a simple, high-level plan for the whole project. Unnecessary detail tends to create wasteful overheads. During project delivery, in monthly initiations, we'll then prepare detailed plans for the upcoming months.'

Mirai left, looking happy as a lark.

Velvety dusk thickened outside the glass walls of the Artophyle office tower. Didi felt tired but at the same time elated and energised with the day's catch.

The deliverables map of a fair-sized construction project by definition presented a maze of configuration items. It carried the danger of miring the project team in detail so that they lost sight of the forest for the trees. Walking this thin line required the sleight of mind that came only with experience.

Getting a competent scheduler who could wade through those depths and deliver precisely to the requirement was a project manager's dream come true.

Didi left the office in a buoyant mood. With the job for the day done, the hurt bones seemed to ache less. The evening was still young, which left time for all kind of adventures of mind and flesh.

Strolling down the boulevard to the police precinct, Didi observed the first cafés opening and dignified flaneurs wearing fedoras and flying scarves unhurriedly pacing the flagstones.

At the precinct, Didi explained to the duty officer the reason for wishing to withdraw the incident report. The phone had miraculously reappeared in the peacoat pocket and the injuries weren't worth of the police's bother.

The duty officer motioned Didi to wait and spoke into a walkie-talkie. A minute or so later, the heavily armoured door leading to the precinct's inner sanctum opened, and a police sergeant in full patrol attire, square and solid as a block of mahogany wood, beckoned Didi inside. Didi followed, without saying a word.

They went up two flights of shabby stairs with creaking steps and splintered wooden banisters. On the landing, city lights glittered merrily through a gothic window of dyed glass panes that showed a tall knight wearing a brass barber's basin for a hat on an emaciated horse slaying a docile-looking dragon.

Leaving the stairs on the first floor, on they went along a corridor laid with scuffed vintage floorboards painted a hundred times over. A heady bouquet made up of stale sweat, gun oil, the acrid bite of propellant and cheap tobacco pervaded the air.

Didi's escort knocked with his truncheon on one of the identical doors that lined the scraped passage wall and opened it for Didi to pass inside. Klebb slouched with elbows planted on the desk and chin buried in the palms. 'You want to take the incident report back, don't you?'

Didi stayed by the door. 'The phone has reappeared. And a few bruises don't make a case.'

Klebb nodded and stood up, absent-mindedly putting one palm on the butt of the service gun in a hip holster. The tiny figure with milk-bottle shoulders offered a stark contrast to the sergeant's fortress-like build. 'You are right. I don't care much about your bruises. And wrong. Your assailant is a career criminal who stole your phone on a contract. A hired gun who has killed before.

'If we nab the bugger on this petty crime, we'll get a chance to have a face-to-face chat. And in such a setting we can be pretty convincing. In all probability, we'll take a dangerous thug off the streets. Make the world safer.'

Didi twisted the edge of the mouth in sceptical doubt.

Klebb sighed. 'OK, if that doesn't fire your boilers, here is another angle for you to consider. Aren't you interested in finding out who put out a contract on you?

'The last time it involved snatching your phone. Apparently, whoever ordered it didn't find it of much use. So, next time it can be snatching you instead of the phone. And if you prove unwilling or unable to satisfy their curiosity, they won't necessarily return you to the phone. As a matter of fact, that'd be a first in my experience. What do you say now?'

Didi hesitated, this turn of the case being completely unexpected. Reluctantly, Didi had to admit that what Klebb said made sense. 'What do you propose?'

Klebb came a few steps nearer, palm still on the gun, looking Didi square in the eye. 'The obvious, actually. It's always the best call to stick with the obvious.

'We keep your report and continue the enquiry. You watch your back. And front, too. I don't have free minders to walk with you. But your agreement to play ball will give me leverage to press the central investigations bureau for favours. Together, there's a good chance we collar the villain. That'll make the world safer. But more importantly, it'll make you safer.'

Back on the street, a wave of tiredness swept over Didi. The whole situation got increasingly entangled by the day. The Metro trains still ran packed, and Didi had to stand grabbing the rail during the whole trip, which wasn't exactly conducive to a mood change.

Back in the apartment, Didi reheated the generous portion of lamb pilaf bought at the Loranca station stalls and slowly ate, washing it down with a pot of green tea. Tasty food had a predictably soothing effect on Didi's spirits. Watching an episode of a mind-numbing series written by a brain-dead playwright further helped to finish off the day on a high note.

* * *

The morning dawned grey and rainy. Didi wore a waxed stockman duster that reached almost to the ground, and succeeded in arriving at work dripping and splashed with mud on the outside but in untarnished sartorial glamour on the inside. In the office, it was all good news.

The top message in the inbox had come from Anan.

> Morning, Didi. I ran the project description past the boss and got zero feedback. Consider it approved. Anan

In no time, Mirai happily trotted up to Didi's desk and, without preamble, unfurled a roll of paper the size of a double bed, packed with tiny boxes. 'Good morning, Didi. Here is the project schedule we did with Azar, Monet and Kim. Even the illustrious Noor spared us a precious half an hour.'

For a moment, Didi remained speechless. 'Holy moly' seemed a fair assessment of the work done by Mirai in the space of a few hours. Finding voice, Didi decided to hide admiration and instead display wry scepticism. 'Didn't we agree that you'll produce only the high-level schedule?'

But Mirai sported a Teflon coat. 'You are absolutely right, Didi. And here it is.' With a magician's flair, Mirai fished out a single sheet seemingly out of the sleeve.

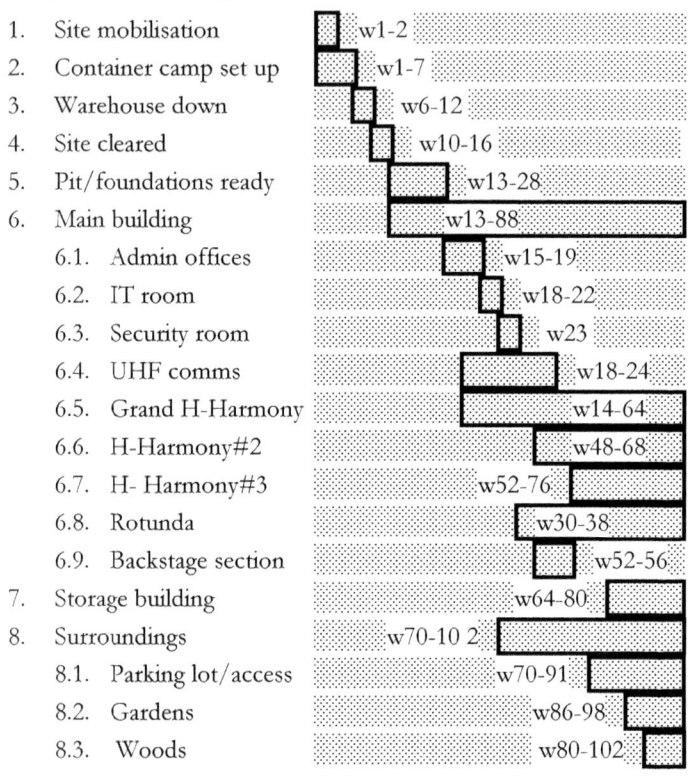

1. Site mobilisation — w1-2
2. Container camp set up — w1-7
3. Warehouse down — w6-12
4. Site cleared — w10-16
5. Pit/foundations ready — w13-28
6. Main building — w13-88
    6.1. Admin offices — w15-19
    6.2. IT room — w18-22
    6.3. Security room — w23
    6.4. UHF comms — w18-24
    6.5. Grand H-Harmony — w14-64
    6.6. H-Harmony#2 — w48-68
    6.7. H- Harmony#3 — w52-76
    6.8. Rotunda — w30-38
    6.9. Backstage section — w52-56
7. Storage building — w64-80
8. Surroundings — w70-102
    8.1. Parking lot/access — w70-91
    8.2. Gardens — w86-98
    8.3. Woods — w80-102

'As you can see, it includes only the two top levels of deliverables. I thought it would be useful, though, if it represented an aggregation of the lower-level configuration items.'

Didi studied the schedule for a while, finally nodding. 'Yeah… I think that'd do for the upfront plan. The detailed plan, on the other hand, is just work-in-progress at this stage. We'll add even more details during the monthly initiations. I can see that the total duration doesn't look too bad, either.'

Mirai looked Didi straight in the eye to break the not-so-good news. 'Our initial assessment has produced the duration of 115 weeks that is nine over the initial estimate. Since there is obviously no way how we can prevail on the global committee to postpone the award ceremony a bit, we planned for the target duration. The good news is, we believe it will be possible to finish in 104 weeks, on condition that we get more people and equipment. That'll increase the cost by some 170 artopools.'

Didi pondered the news for a moment, then shrugged decisively. 'That's nothing unusual, after all. Proposing options is perfectly all right. The role of the project sponsor involves more than serving as an adornment. Have you also prepared a budget estimate?'

Mirai made several more sheets of paper materialise out of thin air. 'We agreed on a rough estimate for the cost of each deliverable in the map. The total is 935 artopools.'

Didi looked up in surprise. 'But that's much higher than the original estimate!'

Mirai sounded apologetic. 'I know, the target listed in the project description is 800 artopools. But we've checked several times, and it's better we stay realistic and not raise false expectations from the very start.'

Didi resisted giving in to arm-twisting, polite and considerate as it felt. 'You've looked for cost-lowering options, haven't you?'

Mirai nodded energetically. 'We have, indeed. The only realistic and effective option for reducing costs we could come up with is to use normal concrete with a coloured finish on top of it, instead of using self-coloured concrete. That could bring the cost back to 850 artopools.'

Didi looked relieved. 'The more options, the better. Now, what we have at the moment is 850 artopools and 115 weeks switching to normal concrete, or adding 170 artopools to reduce the duration to 104 weeks. Sticking with self-coloured concrete will add another 85 artopools on top of either option. I guess the whole idea of using self-coloured concrete sprouted from Noor's artistic mind.

'Anyway, we'll present all the options so that Anan can choose in order to make an informed go/no-go decision towards the end of project initiation. Well done, Mirai! That was a lot of work, but I'm easily satisfied with such an excellent result.'

A06 - Identify risks and plan responses

SOUTH OF THE RIVER, the shallow wash of unpretentious stubby apartment blocks gradually thinned before finally splashing up against a steep range. On top of that spread high prairies that stretched for hundreds of square kilometres, covered mostly with tall and dense grass interrupted here and there by solitary fields. Local dwellers called it 'pampa' in their rolling dialect.

The area adjacent to the drop down to Artopolis was occupied by its satellite city, Pucará. Migrants from the poor tropics and beyond inhabited it, supplying Artopolis with all kinds of cheap labour. And Artopolis was never satiated with devouring it.

Artopolis folk rarely ventured up to Pucará. That place ran by its own rules that remained beyond the grasp of those uninitiated in their ways. And breaking those rules, even unintentionally, could easily result in a traumatic experience.

Not a forgiving place, Pucará. It never hesitated to make a bloody point to keep trespassers away from its boundaries.

Halfway up the face of the cliff, a twilight zone was maintained by consent of the respective powers, where the two worlds met to transact business or, for that matter, pleasure. There, the honour codes of Pucará did not rigidly apply to off-worlders, and the laws of Artopolis got thinned to the max, like the booze sold at street stalls. It was to those troubled and dangerous districts where Didi was heading on a full-moon night.

Swishing through the empty streets on a noiseless e-scooter, Didi pretended to be a ghoul in search of lost souls. It felt cool though mildly ridiculous but more importantly helped to pull together the guts for a face-to-face meeting with Che, a feared, notorious bacrim leader and a figure of significant standing in the two cities' criminal underworld.

Their association started many years back when Che, at the time a fledgling hoodlum, conned Didi, then a fledgling wheeler-dealer, into a scam that in the end left both singed and scarred. At the stand-off, instead of opting for a seemingly wiser decision to scatter to the four winds, they had stood back-to-back and fought it out against crazy odds. Insane as it had looked at the time, it very possibly thwarted the intention of their counterparts in the scam to hunt them down and take out one after the other. In a rare gesture of gratitude, Che had then pledged everlasting loyalty to Didi.

Shortly after, their paths had forked. While Didi was following a limping project manager's career, Che had rapidly risen to fame, growing into one of the underworld's living myths. Over the years, they had met only a couple of times.

But now Didi felt the time was ripe to collect on the debt of their youth.

So, they were on essentially friendly terms. Well, kind of. But when dealing with a career criminal, one could never be certain of one's standing. That's why Didi's guts twisted with a tug of apprehension.

It was getting to three in the morning. Didi parked the rented scooter at the last collection point and continued on foot, climbing the stairs that connected terraces. The higher above Artopolis, the more crowded the streets got. There in the fusion zone, little menace or malice was on open display. Everyone pretended to be everyone's best friend. And if most pucareños carried a fan knife hidden in some deep pocket of their baggy attire, so what?

Fires burned on a large square in front of a dilapidated church, the only flat area among the densely built terraces. Elephantine cast iron vats simmered on the log fires. One contained a thick brew made from lamb heads and intestines with plenty of yucca, camote and choclo. The other offered a lighter and more delicate broth of chicken fragments, rice and yellow ají. While men preferred the former, women tended to favour the latter.

At around half four, the plaza started filling up. The shift of night labourers ascending from Artopolis made a pit-stop to refuel before continuing their arduous climb. They met with the flock of day labourers descending to Artopolis, who had left their homes shortly after midnight and were ready to fill up for the day that lay ahead of them. A smattering of comparatively colourless artopolisians completed the picture.

Loud banter, yelling and blasphemous swearing came from all direction in a dialect Didi didn't quite understand. Jostling for space, Didi got a bowl of soup and hustled a short-legged stool to sit on. Suddenly, a bubble of space and hushed conversation formed all around.

Night shadows shifted and Che appeared out of thin air, silent as a night owl, squatting in front of Didi. 'It's a rare delight to meet you, pal. How is family? Is life treating you well? Do you perchance come to chew the fat with me? Or is it a purely social visit?'

Didi smiled, genuinely pleased with experiencing this blast from the past. 'Greetings, Che. Still keeping to the shadows? I'm doing fine, thank you. My days are getting samey, though, and I feel like I have forgotten the taste of the authentic Ab Gusht.'

Che smiled in a touchingly solemn way. 'You stay true to your roots, Didi; that's commendable. What's on your mind, my friend? Speak up.'

Didi chewed on the soup for a while. According to the Pucará custom, pauses in the conversation showed tactfulness and respect. 'The other day, I got knocked down and my phone got stolen. Next day, I found it in the pocket of my peacoat. The police say they looked at the video footage and could identify the offender, who is a known hired gun. Can you arrange it so that we could meet and I get the opportunity to ask some questions?'

Che remained motionless as if lost in deep thought. Then shrugged. 'No, can't do that. In broad terms, your nemesis is one of us. I can't deliver one of our own to you. That would be a breach of honour'.

Didi kept eyes glued to the bowl, spooning the soup and munching in silence.

Che minutely twitched one corner of the mouth in a shadow of an appreciative grimace, showing delight in Didi's patience and humility. 'But I'm willing to ask your questions on your behalf. What do you want to know?'

Didi raised the eyes to lock them with Che's. 'Why me? Who put out a contract? What comes next? Provided you find him. Or her.'

Che frowned in mock anger. 'Do not insult my intelligence, my friend. If anyone could hide from me that would ruin my reputation. And without a reputation, you are nothing, a pail filled with gristle. But it may take a few days. You know, we crooks tend to stay secretive about our ways. But you'll hear from me.'

Didi nodded. Che stood up and pressed Didi down on the shoulder. 'Don't bother to stand up to give me a hug. Finish your soup; that's a more serious business. I hope we'll meet again one day. I'll always honour my pledge to you.'

The bubble burst, and the pressure of the crowd resumed. Didi pushed the soup bowl with some decent leftovers towards a group of street dogs that silently and patiently waited nearby. A huge wolfdog the size of a calf calmly approached and started eating. Didi fearlessly wiped greasy hands on its matted and stringy hair. That was the custom. And the dogs knew to observe it as well as people did.

A rather mild and generally pleasant morning broke, with a friendly sun generously illuminating Didi's path leading back down to the city. Tuctucs already ran at full throttle and Didi easily made it back to the apartment with enough time remaining to take a shower and change into office attire. A stomach full of night soup made a refuelling stop at the station food stalls redundant. Didi only grabbed a cup of cardamom-flavoured jitter juice without breaking stride and dove into the Metro.

* * *

The day's promise of fun was fulfilled early on with a fabulous turnout for the risk formulation workshop that corresponded to Activity A06 in the project initiation sequence – Identify risks and plan responses. Attendance included Anan and, as a consequence, other department heads had found it difficult to ignore Didi's invitation. Artophyle's chief architect, the venerable Noor, also present, sat quietly at some distance from the group and appeared to be dozing. The project team expectedly assembled in full force.

Facilitating a workshop with the participation of different management levels involved a balancing act. Directors tended to try to dominate the discussion, effectively stifling inputs from the ranks. Conducting separate workshops for managers and technical professions tended to help identify a larger number of technical risks but, at the same time, reduced the diversity of risk types. Conducting two workshops also resulted in the duplication of the related project manager's time expenditure. Didi's firm preference thus involved braving the torment and putting lions and lambs in the same boat.

As a warm-up, Didi threw in the risk that projects delivered for external customers were considered likely to command priority access to Artophyle's limited resources. This risk had been identified very early but was still lacking allocation of the custodian.

Anan at once caught on to the drift. 'Put it on my tab.'

ID: R-001

Cause: HAHAP doesn't have an external customer.

Effect: Company policy establishes that internal departments give priority to projects with external customers (to keep the customers satisfied), and as a result, queue HAHAP requirements.

Impact: HAHAP execution may exceed the agreed time tolerance and result in a lower-quality product.

Response: Strong sponsorship/continuous monitoring of the situation/getting all the executives involved in the project

Custodian: Anan

Status: open.

Didi saved it in the follow-up register. 'It seems we've got off to a flying start. Any more risks?'

There followed a torrent of suggestions. Didi had nothing to worry about. The executives just sat back in an effort to absorb the gush of opinions. No change could be observed in Noor's posture. That is, until somebody mentioned that the HAHAP design resembled a medieval fortress with all towers, cornices and buttresses having just a few slits for windows. It could well result in a deficit of natural light in the grand vestibule, creating a rather depressing atmosphere of a dungeon.

Noor woke up, emitting a delicate cough. 'If that is the complete sum of your anxieties, I'll happily put them to rest. I appreciate the freedom of opinions on artistic subjects that laymen love to cherish, unencumbered by subject knowledge. But with all due respect, and correct me if I am wrong, this project is supposed to manage the realisation of the design that has already passed a peer review and been endorsed by the Artophyle board. I regard this not as an appropriate forum or an opportune moment to reopen those discussions.'

Imani, director of the design department, nodded vigorously. 'The business case has been effectively approved by the Artophyle board. It remains open to eventual changes, of course, to ensure the project's continued business justification. But in this group, I suggest we better focus on threats to project delivery.'

'Hear, hear', directors echoed under their breath.

Mirai cast a furtive glance at Didi, and though receiving nothing in the way of encouragement, decided to make a dash for it. 'I can see another issue with the design. All the walls are made of exposed concrete, which means, the halls will have poor acoustic properties. That will particularly affect the Great Hall of Harmony. It will echo like a cavern. As a consequence, acoustic treatment specified in the design may not be enough, resulting in higher project cost. And besides, the type of treatment required to amend the acoustics may harm the internal aesthetics.'

Noor rolled up the eyelids and put hands together palm to palm in a gesture of silent prayer. 'My dear young colleague insists on adding insult to injury. I doubt that such zeal is called for. After all, it is not by mere happenstance that the project team includes a colleague from the design department - Azar. If project delivery generates any requirement for design modification, Azar will escalate it to Imani and myself and we'll take care of it. It makes little sense to me to try to anticipate every risk under the sun while still being in project initiation.'

Mirai suffered through the bashing, keeping a stubborn scowl but without putting up any resistance. Didi decided it was getting time to calm the heating tempers. 'Could I then suggest a higher-level risk that could serve as a place-holder of sorts?'

ID: R-002

Cause: Project delivery may create a requirement for the fine-tuning of the design.

Effect: Modified/additional deliverables and substitution of materials.

Impact: A potential for the breaching of cost and time tolerances.

Response: Monitor project delivery with a focus on identifying specific risks that will require the modification of design and as a consequence, the updating of the project business case.

Custodian: Azar

Status: open

'I'm confident that the venerable Noor will be willing to admit that little if anything remains etched in stone on a construction project. Particularly, one involving such extent of innovation and conceptual audacity.'

Imani fidgeted on the chair. Noor frowned. Both kept their mouths zipped.

The discussion quickly ebbed. No one thought it made much sense racking their brains to anticipate risks to project delivery. They knew from experience that once the project was launched, there'd be no shortage of material for the follow-up register. They shared in the notion that risk management should involve a degree of proactivity. But each management block included in P3.express tended to generate its own level of risks.

In project initiation, it made sense to keep the focus on higher-level risks. At the time of monthly initiations, operational risks became prominently visible. At the same time, though the project manager knew from experience that plenty of things would go wrong, and there was no way of predicting, which precisely. Proactive risk planning could offer only a partial remedy. The second leg of the project manager's tradecraft focused on anti-fragility.

So, hardly anyone among the workshop participants had inflated expectations for the results. But both the executives and the technical experts still considered it good use of their time as it helped to nurse the budding team spirit. They were all in the same boat and whether the project ended in success or failure depended on everyone.

A07 – Have project initiation peer reviewed

IT WAS GETTING toward nine in the evening when Didi finished with the day's paperwork. Right after the workshop, Didi switched immediate attention to Activity A07 - Have project initiation peer reviewed. It aimed to discover and mitigate the project team's biases. The team and, in particular, the project manager being too close to the work blurred their eye, preventing them from seeing some of the issues. Equally important, the peer review presented an opportunity for fellow project managers to learn from each other's work.

Didi decided to approach Tiam, the veteran project manager famed for being highly experienced. If Didi was certain about one thing, it was that Tiam wouldn't shrink from saying the blunt truth about Didi's work. Peer reviews occasionally produced little beyond ego-petting, reflecting a fear that the reviewee might take criticism personally. And what went around, came around.

Tiam occupied a desk in the far corner of the same floor, and Didi marched straight to it without any prior announcement. Tiam sat on a floormat in the passage with headphones playing some mantra music, practising levitation. Didi crept up from behind and tapped Tiam on the shoulder.

Tiam rolled over onto the back and lashed out with one leg, aiming to connect with the unknown assailant. Didi knew the routine and easily sidestepped the kick, the inertia of which carried through, making Tiam do a backward roll that ended with a crash-landing on the knees. Didi lightly stepped in front, though remaining ready to pivot and feint if necessary.

But Tiam – untypically - affected a sombre mood that impeded the continuation of horseplay. 'Hey Didi, pal, you're getting more agile by the day.'

Didi still danced lightly like a bantam-weight boxer, just in case it was another ruse. 'Cheers, Tiam; I am just a patient scholar of your deadly skills. Learning from you is as exciting as befriending a cobra. How is you floating, mate?'

Tiam smirked. 'Watch your language, Didi. It's not floating, pal; it's levitation. Want me to spell it for you?'

Didi saw through this weak attempt at distraction and laughed. 'Since you opt for discussing conceptual subtleties, I guess you haven't been able yet to get even an inch of clearance between your butt and the floor.'

Tiam sighed forlornly, looking at Didi with mock disdain. 'It's not all black and white, old chum. First, you need to learn how to soar in your mind, and only then your mind's wings will carry the weight of your body. Disco ergo sum. I learn, therefore I am. You've mentioned in passing that you were a scholar of my ways. What teaching have you come for this time?'

Tiam nimbly rose from the knees and took the chair by the desk. Didi sat on the desk proper, feet dangling. Aping churlishness tended to win Tiam's attention. 'Last week, on our way to Sanriol, the boss appointed me as the project manager for the Halls of Harmony project. Now it's time for our project initiation peer review. Can you do it for me?'

Tiam clearly saw through Didi's modest bid at fame. But whatever the angle, the fact that Didi had effectively flown in Rilke's company jet commanded a degree of respect. 'Sure, oh my high-flying Didi. No problem, send me the project documentation. Let me take a look, then we'll sit down for a chat and I'll send you my feedback in no time. Oh, and I'll need on file your permission to talk to your stakeholders.'

'Of course. I'll also let them know that you might call, so that they keep their lawyers on standby.' Didi hopped off the desk. 'And don't give up on the floating.'

The phone pinged with an incoming message, displaying a link to a darknet messenger. That piqued Didi's curiosity. Taking a seat in the floor lounge to avoid prying colleagues creeping up unobserved, while obscured by partitions and miscellaneous office furniture, Didi went through the messenger's onion layers.

It felt like, well, may be like sliding down a dark funnel, producing a strangely unnerving effect. Didi had no interests in darknet and didn't enjoy this first delve. But there certainly had to be a good reason for such extreme precautions.

Finally, a text message opened. Che had sent it. Who else?

> The contract for the hit on you is competently layered and going through the layers took time. A Sanriol criminal operator going by the name of Pollin issued it. The contract involved snatching your phone. When approached for details, Pollin cooperated, naming as the requestor a joe from the office of the chairman of Sanriol corporate bankers' association. When gently squeezed, the latter admitted acting on request from an aide of a visiting CEO called Rilke who presumably originated the contract. Hope that sheds enough light on the matter so that you can take the necessary precautions. Keep well, my friend.

To say that the message stunned Didi would have been the understatement of the century. To hell with the century - of the millennium. None of it made sense. Were any precautions necessary? But attempting to protect oneself against something that made no sense made no sense either. What a poser.

On an impulse, Didi called Klebb to set up a meeting, and then Mirai, to ask to hold the fort for a while. Walking in big, purposeful strides, Didi covered the short distance to the police citadel in record time.

A different sergeant, with broad shoulders and a boxer's kind face, led the familiar way to Klebb's office. One of the detectives dozed on a threadbare couch. Another pounded on the keyboard with two thick fingers, typing up some kind of a report. Klebb sat with feet, in scuffed imitation leather sneakers worn down at the heels, propped on the scarred desk. A gumshoe icon.

When Didi entered, Klebb didn't bat an eyelid, much less alter posture. Didi didn't bother to sit down. 'I'm withdrawing my report.'

One edge of Klebb's mouth twitched in a smirk. 'You sure? That'll deliver you to the villains, then.'

Didi shrugged in a display of nonchalance that was almost genuine. 'I don't care. Che sarà sarà.'

Klebb shrugged back. 'Your call, pal.'

Didi exited the police building with a sensation of liberation. Though, come to think of it, there was pretty little to feel elated about. If Che's sources were accurate, Rilke had set Didi up for a snatch while they were still enjoying the high life in Zourbagan. That circumstance baffled Didi no end. But somehow, life still felt good when strolling down the boulevard.

Didi briefly toyed with the idea of going back to the office, but instead took a chair in one of the street cafes and passed time watching flaneurs and mulling the conundrum of the Sanriol conspiracy over glass after sweating glass of the vibrantly hued Aperol. Time passed at a trot.

The melodious ping of the phone resonated pleasantly in the gathering violet dusk. Didi reluctantly swiped the screen to see a message from Tiam.

> Didi, chum, where the hell are you hiding from me? It's still well before midnight and you are not at your desk. What's cooking, pal, are you getting delusions of power, or what?
>
> I've read the documents and interviewed stakeholders. Let's have a chat, comrade. Meet me tomorrow at six in the morning, as my schedule gets really dense later in the day.

Didi groaned inwardly, feeling a mild stirring of annoyance. Tiam's legendary competence bowed only to unbelievable efficiency. Didi should have known that and returned to the office. Now, to keep the six o'clock appointment would require a serious effort. Didi drained the glass, got up from the table and headed straight for bed.

* * *

Next morning, Didi achieved no mean feat by getting to the office without really waking up. At least Metro trains ran half-full at that hour, and Didi could snooze sitting on the springy bench. Tiam, in comparison, looked energetic, vibrating with the anticipation of putting in another day of finest work.

Giving Didi a once-over seemed to raise Tiam's spirits another few degrees. 'Morning Didi. I suggest you grab yourself a chair since in your state of negative wakefulness you may fall off the desk, if you perch on it.

'So, I've checked the project description, deliverables map and follow-up register, browsed through the schedule, and also talked to some of your stakeholders.

'It seems that you have a strong and involved sponsor, don't you?'

Didi gave a noncommittal shrug. 'So far so good, and it makes me happy. But we've travelled only a short distance yet.'

Tiam twirled a dreadlock around a finger. 'I hope it's only about the high-level aspects of the project. Otherwise, you know, it can get a little stifling.'

Didi couldn't have agreed more. 'It's OK, Anan has never tried to micromanage me. We haven't had any critical issues that required Anan's intervention so far. But I keep the sponsor generally in the loop and beyond that ask to take the routine, high-level decisions.'

Tiam forgot about the dreadlocks and was vigorously taking notes. 'How about the content of the Project Description then?'

Didi was still not sufficiently awake to understand where the questions led. 'Sure, that's one of the routine, high-level decisions that I've just mentioned. I asked Anan to check and approve it.'

Tiam nodded vigorously. 'That's just about perfect. And what about the deliverables map and the schedule?'

Didi showed a bit of surprise. 'No, I didn't ask Anan to approve them; I just sent the documents for information. Did I have to ask for formal approval?'

Tiam shook the head sending dreadlocks into a frenzied swinging. 'Not really. The deliverables map and follow-up register are not considered to be as high-level as the project description. Accordingly, there is no need to get them formally approved by the sponsor unless you see a benefit in it. But it's perfectly appropriate to share their final drafts with Anan for information, to keep the sponsor in the loop, as you've put it.

'Were there any other important issues during the project initiation that needed Anan's decision?'

Gradually, the ristretto Didi sipped got traction and cleared the mind of the early-morning fog. 'Well, the cost/duration balance of the project seemed a bit out of whack. The project team has prepared several options that I'll present to Anan in Activity A08 towards the end of project initiation when a go/no-go decision will be due.'

Tiam nodded, ticking items on the tablet. 'Now, last but not least, have you set up a well-structured way of storing project documentation?'

For Didi, that felt like falling off a log. 'HAHAP uses a cloud storage facility that is perfectly secure since Artophyle has been assigned a dedicated cloud server. I've set up a separate directory for the project, and all the project documents go there. The facility has its own versioning system that we use for minor updates, and at specific times, I store a separate snapshot for approved documents.

'All project team members have write access to all documents except the project description, which only I have write access to. All executives and line managers in the company have read access to the documents.'

Tiam nodded one last time. 'All right, here is my verdict. The documents are well-written and clear. The schedule seems on par with the rest. What I could glean from the latter is that you've delegated the whole scheduling process. As Mirai is definitely competent in the matter, it's fine, as long as you supervise both the process and the result. You can delegate work, but not the responsibility for the result.

'I'm less supportive of your designating Mirai as the point for the identification of project options to balance duration and cost. Mirai took the right path talking to other team members, but it's best that you're fully involved and lead those discussions yourself. Project options are serious stuff. You'll present them for Anan's consideration as if they were your own. Are you sure that those picked up by Mirai are exhaustive?'

This last remark caught Didi a bit off balance. It now appeared an essential task of project initiation had been given superficial treatment. 'Thank you, Tiam for drawing my attention to the matter. That's a risk, isn't it? Let's add it to the follow-up register right away.'

> **ID: R-003**
>
> **Cause:** During the peer review of project documentation, the reviewer (Tiam) observed that the project manager had delegated the identification of cost/duration options to an inexperienced project team member.
>
> **Effect:** It is possible that the identified options are not exhaustive.
>
> **Impact:** Project delivery will be based on a suboptimal set of options presented for the sponsor's review and approval.
>
> **Response:** The project manager will conduct a follow-up workshop with the project team to ensure that none of essential options have been overlooked.
>
> **Custodian:** Didi
>
> **Status:** Open.

Tiam looked delighted with this solution. 'That takes care of it. Send me the link to the project's health register and give write access so that I can fill in the peer review form.'

It was still not yet eight in the morning when Didi took up position behind the desk. Realising the need to put a limit to the delegation zeal, Didi personally sent team members a summons to join the meeting at nine. That left enough time to go up to the rooftop cafeteria and consume a bowl of Scottish porridge flavoured with fresh ginger and stewed plums.

Sasha, Azar and Monet arrived on the dot of nine. Kim sent a message asking to be excused due to the department director's explicit instructions to concentrate on the regular job. That looked like a challenge that needed to be addressed straight away.

> Good morning, Anan.
>
> Upon completion of the peer review earlier today, I called an urgent meeting of the project team to revisit project options that have been identified at an earlier stage. The reviewer expressed a concern that they didn't look exhaustive. All project team members are at the moment with me except Kim who asked to be excused on Eka's orders. I take it as another demonstration of the openly obstructive attitude to HAHAP by the director of mechanical engineering department. Could I kindly ask you to intervene.
>
> Kind regards,
> Didi.

Still smarting from Eka's affront, Didi launched into the meeting. 'I apologise for the urgency, but we need to manage a risk identified during the peer review. Tiam remained unconvinced that project options had been explored in sufficient depth. If I were the one who led the discussions, I would have been able to dispel Tiam's concerns. Since I had chosen to delegate this task to Mirai, I was in no position to do so. I plead guilty to Tiam's charge.

'So, let's go again through the options that you have picked with Mirai and see if we can add to those. The HAHAP performance targets are 800 artopools for cost and twenty-four months for duration.

'The project budget plus management reserve is 1,000 artopools and the board could conceivably agree to a top-up. The project time tolerance is twenty-nine months. Here, no top-ups appear feasible as the award ceremony is scheduled to take place in thirty months.

'These are the known options that I have reworked a bit for consistency.

'850 artopools, normal concrete, twenty-nine months.

'935 artopools, self-coloured concrete, twenty-nine months.

'1,020 artopools, normal concrete, twenty-four months

'1,105 artopools, self-coloured concrete, twenty-four months.'

With peripheral vision, Didi noted a door open a notch and Kim peer through the crack, carefully eying the setting for clues. 'Come in Kim. Good that you could join us. You haven't missed much; we've just kicked off.'

The whole of Kim's slight frame slid through the door. 'Look, I'm sorry, but Eka is absolutely adamant that department staff must concentrate on department priorities. There has been such a shout-out with Anan that my ears withered. I got marching orders to join you this one time but the outlook for the future remains grim. Eka won't hesitate to nail me to the boards if I don't deliver in accordance with the department plan. And I see no way of cloning myself.'

Didi switched to diaphragmatic breathing to control the irritation spike. 'Let's solve problems as they come. Anyway,

I'm curious what it is that obsesses Eka so much and does not affect other departments to a degree that even comes close to such theatrics?'

Kim shuffled feet and nervously cleared the throat before speaking. 'Well, you know, it's supposed to be confidential, need-to-know and all that.'

Irritation was getting the better of Didi. 'Kim, don't you think need-to-know is exactly what describes my interest in the matter? Or would you prefer me to call Anan to confirm it?'

Kim raised the hands in mock self-defence. 'OK, OK, don't shoot the messenger. Rilke is chin-deep in negotiating a terabuck contract in Sanriol and we run support around the clock. It will require putting up high-volume production plants at the site, like for pouring huge tonnage of concrete or churning out gigantic cable harnesses, and that's just for starters. Guys, it's more complex than building a Death Star.'

Swallowing that bit down appeared problematic; it needed chewing up first and Didi pushed it aside. 'Right, now I see it belongs in Anan's league. Let's return to the matter in hand.'

Kim raised a hand cautiously. 'There is this nutty idea of putting up a wind farm on top of the Hall of Harmony. It's sort of aped from the Strata tower in London, the marvel of ecological architecture. We estimate it will cost some 160 artopools and can be in all probability achieved within the twenty-nine months.

'The upside is, it will sure create a landmark skyline and possibly push down a bit the electricity bill. On the downside, I as an engineer have my doubts about its utility. The turbines will cause vibration that will be felt throughout the building, despite shudder-abatement measures. The turbines on the Strata tower span for one whole day before getting shut down.

'And besides, Artopolis is not really a windy city.'

Monet picked up the hot potato without showing much enthusiasm for it. 'The wind farm will require installing some additional electrical gear. Wind turbines produce so-called wild power, which is AC with both voltage and frequency unregulated due to surges in rotor revolutions.

'Wild AC needs to be converted to DC and then to commercial AC, the voltage and frequency-regulated AC that can flow into the building grid. We estimate it will add some eighty-five artopools to the wind farm cost.

'Whether we can fit it into twenty-nine months will depend to a large extent on the work discipline of Eka's shop. If they keep to the schedule, we'll do our part in time. If they pig it up, there is no float in our planning that'll allow to absorb the slippage.'

Didi raised an eyebrow at Kim, who shrugged, eyes cast down on twiddling thumbs. Didi inhaled to lungs bursting, then pushed the air out with a loud swoosh. 'OK, it's a risk.'

ID: R-004

Cause: There is no guarantee that the mechanical engineering department will stick to the schedule of wind farm construction.

Effect: Slippage will delay the input of the electrical engineering department.

Impact: Wind farm installation may be not completed within the project time tolerance of twenty-nine months.

> **Response:** The project manager will monitor the execution of the wind farm work package based on weekly checkpoint reports by Kim as supplier representative on the project team.
> **Custodian:** Didi
> **Status:** Open.

Didi looked around the table. 'Any other suggestions? None? Good, as too many options may confuse Anan.

'That's it, then. Thanks for your time and Kim, please pass my deep respects on to Eka.'

Kim scurried out of the room ahead of the others. Mirai stayed behind, a bit hesitantly, getting ready for receiving yet another bashing. But Didi had accepted that delegating option identification to Mirai had been a mistake. And mistakes were an integral part of project management. The important thing was to recognise and correct them quickly. 'Stand easy, Mirai. I pronounce you not guilty.'

Mirai visibly relaxed and resumed breathing. 'But what about the extra treatment that may be required to improve the poor acoustics? Remember, I raised this issue at the first workshop.'

Mirai's tenacity caught Didi on the wrong foot. 'Don't push it Mirai, I can still reconsider my verdict on your case. And stop thinking you are a pit bull. Let go. We'll deal with it when it happens. If it happens. If Anan approves the wind farm, it'll likely have a devastating impact on acoustics anyway and require a major redesign.'

Mirai nodded and left, albeit still a bit grudgingly to Didi's vigilant eye. It was getting on noon, but the morning porridge still warmed Didi's tummy, and there was no time to be lost.

A08 - Take a go/no-go decision

PROJECT INITIATION slowly drew to its end. Activity A08 involved the sponsor taking the go/no-go decision. It meant either confirming the project's start, sending it back to the drawing board, or completely rejecting it.

Artophyle projects that included external customers observed this gate without exception. Internal projects often lacked this step, slinking into existence without a clear decision. But the importance of creating a clear gate also for launching internal projects that put in proper commitments prior to commencing project delivery gradually dawned on the Artophyle board.

During the fat times, Artophyle had readily invested in just about any project. The availability of easy money increased Artophyle's risk appetite. But for several years, the tide had turned and throwing money around went out of vogue. The 'go' decision effectively confirmed the existence of a business justification for the project.

Over the last years, Artophyle had started introducing a portfolio management system that allowed evaluation of project proposals in a balanced holistic way compatible with the company's strategies. After a while, it had become increasingly evident that many of the more recent project failures had had their roots in portfolio management.

One classical mistake involved running too many projects in parallel. As a result, the executives had recently become much more difficult to convince of a project's merits. 'No-go' decisions ceased to be stigmatised as the organisation's failures. Rather, a culture of accepting them as a sieve that passed only those projects that provided top benefits for Artophyle had emerged. Introducing a structured approach to project initiation had been pivotal in achieving this turnaround in corporate attitudes.

It was thus with an easy heart that Didi wrote to the sponsor.

> Anan,
>
> Since we're approaching the end of the project initiation, could I kindly ask to take the go/no-go decision regarding HAHAP.
>
> To ensure that your decision is an informed one, please find below the options related to cost and time tolerances, which the project team could identify. Some of these exceed approved cost and/or time tolerances.
>
> - 850 artopools, 29 months normal concrete, no wind farm.
> - 1,020 artopools, 24 months, normal concrete, no wind farm.

- 1,095 artopools, 29 months, normal concrete, wind farm.

- 935 artopools, 29 months, self-coloured concrete, no wind farm.

- 1,105 artopools, 24 months, self-colored concrete, no wind farm.

- 1,180 artopools, 29 months, self-coloured concrete, wind farm.

The latest versions of the project description, deliverables map, follow-up register, health register and schedule are attached for ease of reference.

I'm waiting for your decision.

Kind regards,

Didi

Despite it being well past lunch time, Didi went to old flame the vending machine in the lounge for the staple granola bar. But standing before it, Didi committed an act of cowardly betrayal and instead went up to the roof cafeteria to a proper lunch with a view.

Up in the Artophyle Sky Lounge, Didi absorbed the rather drab Artopolis roofscape stretching under an only marginally more inspiring sky of asphalt hue, while indulging in a smoked salmon pizza sprinkled with a dash of caramelised red onions, cheese substituted with crème fraiche. In contrast to the view outside, this faux-Puck creation looked and tasted equally exquisite.

Didi had no feeling of elation or achievement, just of hard work diligently completed. Then Didi's thoughts took a sharp turn and predictably focused on Eka and the Sanriol project.

Not that Didi could blame Eka for the atrocious disrespect for HAHAP. Department directors sat in hot chairs and had to toe the CEO line. Besides, Artophyle did not survive on charity donations, and revenue-generating projects also paid Didi's own comfortable salary. The Sanriol job, if Rilke managed to squeeze the money out of the Global Development Bank's fat purse, would keep the company afloat for the better part of the next decade.

The problem was, the project's galactic demands dwarfed Artophyle's capacities and recourse to human talent. Before Rilke had angled the Sanriol project that was now being reeled in, HAHAP looked like a five-star job. Didi still vividly remembered the efforts at romancing the mayor's scheme and all the surrounding cooing, tutting and brutal bashing of the competition. Now, the prospective Zourbagan job cast a shadow that all but eclipsed HAHAP's glitter.

And it could be expected to get only worse. Zourbagan would hoover up all of Artophyle's resources, leaving Didi in the lurch. Frantic as it sounded, HAHAP had no future. Anan couldn't fail to realise it. Starting HAHAP before it got firmly anchored in the company's portfolio would be a fatal blunder.

As if on cue, Didi's phone pinged with an incoming message.

> Thanks for the information., I'll need to discuss the matter with Rilke and the board before taking the plunge. That can take some time. I'll get back to you when I'm ready.
>
> Regards,
> Anan

Didi couldn't see any chance of salvation for the HAHAP but still hoped the project manager's low horizon obscured the larger order of things.

*   *   *

Riding back home on the Metro, Didi by chance caught the vintage train, a few of which were still running. Its carriages had open chain-fenced vestibules, connected by gangways made of overlapping metal plates.

Devoid of roll absorbers, the carriages heaved like a brig in a storm. Didi grasped the thin post that served as anchor for the fence chains with both hands, swaying in sync with the curves of the track. Turbulence caused by the train's passage tousled the warm tunnel air between the carriages. The clang of metal, clickety-clack of wheels on switches and rail squeal echoed back from the narrow tunnel walls, ringing in the ears. Yellow blotches of service lights rushed by like comets in the blackness of the universe.

To make the sensation of time travel completely authentic, Didi only missed the pungent and eye-stinging coal smoke from the engine. But in that respect, the Metro Authority had drawn the line; even their vintage trains had electric drives.

All the way home, Didi kept mentally tossing around the phone-snatching incident. It felt a relief to assume that there seemed to be no obvious reason for looking over the shoulder all the time or to study shop windows in an attempt to pick out a tail. Didi also started to realise both the formidable magnitude of the Sanriol job and the matching calibre of competition. Businessmen have disappeared for less. Much less.

And Didi had landed in the thick of it all by pure coincidence. It seemed a safe bet that Rilke had never intended to drag Didi along all the way to Zourbagan. But one thing had led to another, and there they were. Didi had certainly not been vetted to brush shoulders with wheeler-dealers at that stratospheric level. Competition was smart and enterprising as hell. Didi's phone could have been slyly bugged.

Or Didi could have been bought on the spot, with the phone compromised knowingly.

Having at last realised the threat Didi potentially posed to the Sanriol job, Rilke had decided to verify its actual dimensions by ordering the snatch. But why go for such drama?

True, if Didi were clean, property control could simply reclaim the phone under some innocent pretext and pass it on to the in-house IT experts to check it out.

But if Didi had been turned, such tactic would misfire, likely leading to the elimination of incriminating evidence before turning in the phone.

As it happened, the phone had turned out to be clean and Didi exonerated. Physical damage had been minimal – a fine professional was at work - but together with the return of the phone sufficient to camouflage the true motive behind the attack.

Added up, it all made sense. Well, kind of. But Didi felt there still might be a very different explanation for the incident. The snatch could have a pile of other meanings.

All those doubts and uncertainties exerted a pressure on the psyche, and Didi was spiralling into depression. In an effort to shake off bad thoughts, Didi focused on the immediate.

Before the sponsor made the go/no-go decision, the project manager's hands remained bound. This interlude of idleness felt like drifting on the currents and created restlessness of mind and body. The working rhythm built up during project initiation started misfiring.

A09 – Kick off the project

DESPITE DIRE and unpredictable circumstances, Didi decided to go out on a limb and start the preparation of Activity 09 – Kick off the project.

Back at the desk, Didi sketched the meeting's breakdown structure – location, agenda, time slot, catering, entertainment. P3.express insisted that project kick-off should become a memorable event, rather than a boring quickie in the dusty and scuffed conference room. Somehow, Didi didn't feel in the mood for going through all that effort. 'Mirai, haul yourself over here. Let's have a chat.'

Mirai appeared like the genie of the lamp, materialising out of thin air with a Cheshire cat grin. 'Here I am, Master! Your wish is my command!'

Didi managed to keep a straight face though it did take a bit of effort. 'Right, Mirai, it's time to plan the project kick-off meeting.'

Mirai seemed to smell a rat. 'Do you mean Anan has already given the green light? Wow.'

'Not quite "wow" yet,' Didi admitted grudgingly. 'But we'll get it any moment and better be in the starting blocks by then. Let's get cracking.'

Mirai looked satisfied with this reasoning. 'Whom do we invite?'

'The project team members, for sure. Plus, all other stakeholders listed in the project description. And let's invite as many executives and company managers as we can think of.'

A shadow of hesitation flickered across Mirai's face. 'I thought it was only intended for the project team? I can understand the inclusion of listed stakeholders, perhaps, but concerning the rest?'

Didi laughed 'Why are you being so stingy, Mirai?'. 'I had no idea you were a relative of Scrooge. The project kick-off meeting celebrates the project's official launch. That's a great occasion for an Artophyle-wide get-together.

'It'll help us create understanding and gain support for HAHAP; we'll need as many of those executives and managers to help us later on as we can get. Milling with the Artophyle crowd will give us a chance to parade our ambitions and convert more fence-sitters into HAHAP champions.

'And we can't have enough friends, you know; not in a situation when we need to compete for attention and resources with the budding Sanriol operation. Weaving the network takes plenty of time, effort, patience and determination. The kick-off meeting can get us off to a flying start.'

Mirai produced another Cheshire cat grin. 'I'm converted Didi. I'll make a list and send them a planner link to determine the best date. What about the venue and the programme? I mean, you can't possibly zap this crowd's attention with a slide show, or do you think you can?'

'No Mirai, of course I can't. The moment they get bored, they'll leave. And that's precisely the opposite of our plan.' Didi's discourse suddenly snagged on the word 'plan'. 'True, one purpose of the kick-off meeting is to create a broad understanding of the project's objectives. But a more important one is team-building. Whatever venue we choose, one thing it can't be is boring.'

Mirai toyed with a pencil, lost in thought. 'I believe I'm getting the drift. Give me just one minute. It's starting to gel. I'm getting there, I'm getting there. Just another moment, it's coming. Ah-h-h, here it is!

'It's good weather these days, right? So, how about setting up a marquee in front of the old warehouse on the future HAHAP site and having a barbecue?'

Didi was speechless. 'That's... That's crazy! But I love it! Let's do nothing by halves! Let's go full hog! Mirai, you think like a true genie.

'Talk to Elvan from the internal services department to arrange catering, balloons galore and a band, like a klezmer one. Anan will inaugurate the project. I'll make a brief speech about the HAHAP objectives and future benefits. And after that the band will kick in and the networking start. Is it a great plan, or what?'

Mirai nodded solemnly. 'It's an absolutely magnificent plan, oh Master. Could I humbly ask you for the favour of being appointed the custodian of Activity A09, please?'

Didi felt energised by the playfulness of Mirai's tone. 'That's the spirit Mirai. Your request is granted. I truly see it as a win-win situation: you're enjoying taking on more responsibilities, which is an intern's dream come true, and I enjoy giving them away, which is apt for the seasoned project manager that I am.

'As I can delegate the work but not the accountability for the result, I'll be shadowing you much of the time. But if you keep me in the loop, I won't attempt to micromanage you. Promise.

'Feel free to start the preliminary work but wait before entering into commitments until I tell you.'

Mirai broke in a happy grin. 'I'll make you proud of me, oh Master.'

One important aspect of the kick-off event remained to be clarified: who would pick up the tab for it? Didi made a quick reckoning and it came to some six artopools, max. It could be conceivably charged either against the remaining HAHAP cost tolerance agreed by Anan or, being essentially a marketing cost, Anan's own department imprest.

* * *

Feeling an excess of energy, Didi hopped on a velocipede and treadled down to Dockland Marshes to have a closer look at the old company warehouse destined to make space for the Halls of Harmony.

Artopolis stood at the confluence of the Dàhé river with Mar de Tormentas, the Stormy Sea. The port, located in an area known since the dawn of times as the Docklands, came into being in the murky and distant time of the Wagon Trail Wars.

Since then, its size and importance went through several peaks and troughs. Following the receding waterline, caused by more and more water upstream getting diverted to irrigation, the port wharfs and piers had gradually extended into the Dàhé bay to allow the docking of ocean-going vessels.

Older wharfs had decayed and crumbled, surrounding the active port facilities with what became known as the Dockland Marshes, an area of poor neighbourhoods dominated by decaying brownstones, deserted industrial wastelands, potted roads and a generally bad odour.

Block and street names rang with the romance of high-sea adventures: Galleon Wharf that included Curcuma Dock and Vanilla Quay; East Indiaman Wharf with Nutmeg Dock, Cardamom Landing and Clove Quay. It made the contrast with the sad reality even sharper.

A year or so before, the mayor of Artopolis had succeeded in securing Reconstruction and Development Fund money to undertake conversion of the Dockland Marshes into an upscale residential district. To initiate transformation, construction crews had to secure the area block by block. The first haute couture apartment towers and strips of town houses surrounded by designer landscaping had already sprung up in what became the rear-guard, with the construction front slowly pressing on.

The Halls of Harmony project was a piece of that campaign. The old warehouse sat in the Tea Clipper Wharf at the flank of the main construction thrust. A new Metro line was being dug to connect Dockland Marshes with Concorde station on the main line going south from Place Etoile.

The mayor's firm promise to set up a Metro station right next to the Halls of Harmony site had added further lustre to the project's expected benefits. But until then, the construction battleground could be reached only by tuctuc, scooter or velocipede.

It took Didi an hour and a half to treadle to the Tea Clipper Wharf. A wiser approach would have been to take the Metro to Concorde and hop on a tuctuc for the last leg. After several nasty accidents, the city authorities had banned velocipedes from Dàhé tunnels, and crossing the river by ferry junk had eaten up the better part of a half-hour. On the other hand, cruising without hurry in very fine weather put Didi in a buoyant mood.

The old warehouse stood in a lot, overgrown with weeds and ivy. Most of the glassed roof had collapsed like a century ago, and loose, red-brown bricks poured down the walls in cascades of scree. Didi could hear the wind whistling through the broken structure and the rustle of birds or rats scurrying in the dense undergrowth. An urban wilderness.

The ping of an incoming message shattered the idyllic reverie. Didi trotted to the building in search of shadow to shield the phone screen from sunlight. Company phones were not exactly cheap stuff but still lacked in expensive features like AMOLED screens. Didi never complained, since they were free and that's what counted.

> Didi,
>
> After a round of consultations with Artophyle board members, I can confirm my 'go' decision. I approve the option for 1,105 artopools, 24 months duration, self-coloured

> concrete, no wind farm. The project cost tolerance is raised to 1,200 artopools, the time tolerance to 26 months. Bear in mind that the time tolerance is final and won't be upped, come what may.
>
> Anan'

Anan's traction at board level left Didi duly impressed. Given the calibre of folks on the board and the competing priorities they inevitably faced, the turnaround stayed rather on the quick side. The decision made sense, too, which impressed Didi even more.

The project description needed updating with the details of the approved option. Long gone were the days when the rookie Didi had thought that once approved by the sponsor, the project description became etched in stone. Rather, the project description remained a living document, baselined whenever necessary. Otherwise, it would lose its utility.

Didi briefly considered returning to the office, but breathed in the tangy weed aroma and decided to hang out at the warehouse site for a while. Office air made one sick.

Given the overall desolate state of the Dockland Marshes, it offered a surprisingly fast internet connection. Didi rifled the weeds, retrieved an ancient floorboard and using loose bricks as support, improvised a bench.

Resting back against the brick wall of the warehouse warm from the sun produced an uncanny sensation of leaning on an elephant. Didi shook it off, fished a tablet out of the backpack – never leave office without it, at least not during office hours – and played the virtual keys.

Project Description V. 1.0. *(baselined at end of project initiation).*
Project name: Halls of Harmony (HAHAP)
Benefits:

- 4 - Promoting Artophyle Inc.
- 2 - Engaging with the mayor
- 2 - Engaging with the community
- 1 - Having a venue for own events
- 1 - Obtaining revenue from leases

Cost including tolerance: 1,200 artopools
Time including tolerance: 26 months.
Project product requirements and quality expectations:

- Capacity for 5,000 attendees/spectators.
- Multi-functionality.
- Huge backstage area.
- Large storage area.
- Minimalist interior design that can be adapted to different types of events.
- Landmark exterior design.
- Overall climate neutrality.
- Water heating with solar panels.
- Electricity generation with photovoltaic panels

Approved delivery option: 1,105 artopools, 24 months duration, self-coloured concrete, no wind farm.

Stakeholders:

- Anan: sponsor, director of S&M department
- Didi: project manager
- Sasha: project team member, S&M Department staff

- Azar: project team member, design department staff
- Monet: project team member, electrical engineering department staff
- Kim: project team member, mechanical engineering department staff
- Tiam: peer reviewer, project management pool
- Schwartz: Chairman of the Board of ArtoHolding
- Rilke: CEO
- Imani: director of the design department
- Noor: senior architect, design lead
- Eka: director of the mechanical engineering department
- Darci: director of the electrical engineering department.

Didi briefly considered the benefit of sending the new version of the project description for the final formal approval to Anan, but quickly decided against it. Changes only included information transferred from the sponsor's communication of formal approval. Didi saw no need to butter the toast first on one side and then on the other, too.

And finally, Didi gave the thumbs-up to Mirai to proceed with the preparation of the kick-off meeting. It was going on three in the afternoon; high time for grabbing a bite and heading back to the office.

The Dockland Marshes enjoyed little fame for its grub. But being a local, Didi would hardly starve to death anywhere in Artopolis. Crossing the boundary into the Carrack Wharf, Didi treadled down Aniseed Quay until skidding to a halt in front of the 'Almirante Orozimbo Barbosa' tavern to get a plate of unpretentiously delicious deep-fried lamb and beef tucumanas with lots of fire-breathing llajua sauce.

As pushing the treadle on a full stomach felt perverted, Didi activated the propulsion aid and effortlessly cruised the remaining stretch to the Concorde Metro station with its distinctive white obelisk. On the platform, Didi hesitated for a moment. Right track to the office, left track home. The train on the left track arrived first, solving Didi's dilemma. It was not quite four yet, but what the deuce.

* * *

The project kick-off meeting took place a week later. Mirai really pushed the pedal to the metal, raising the pace of preparations to a frenzy. Didi readily admitted being overawed with the effort and the result.

Arriving at the scene ahead of the guests, Didi could barely recognise the site. The weeds were gone and the ground around the warehouse was bulldozed flat and even, and strewn with crushed oxblood brick. An airy white marquee looked as if it was floating in the air at some distance from the crumbling warehouse façade that still bore its Georgian features with impressive dignity.

A barbecue wagon stood to one side, with hickory-flavoured smoke rising merrily from its broad chimney. On a stage to the other side of the warehouse, a band quietly rehearsed tempi. A million balloons in the colours of the Scottish thistle festooned the marquee and warehouse.

The guests started arriving, and soon a sizeable crowd assembled. Didi took it all in from a distance, pleasantly surprised to see all the board in attendance, with the exception of Rilke, who continued shuttling between Sanriol and the HQ of the Global Development Bank in an effort to stitch together funding for the financial district project. Since the board showed up in full strength, most of senior executives followed suit.

Anan climbed onto the bandstand and tapped the mic. 'Good afternoon. Thank you for coming. Today we celebrate the launching of the HAHAP' - some laughter rippled through the crowd – 'oh, my apologies, the Halls of Harmony Project. The board aims to firmly put Artophyle on the world's map and as you may know, we are pursuing different avenues to that end. The Halls of Harmony have been chosen as a bearing point by which to steer. And all of us here, we are in the same boat. Each of us will get an opportunity to contribute to this common undertaking. Here is to us then, the HAHAP crew!'

Some isolated clapping followed, but the enthusiasm for food and music clearly prevailed. Still, the kick-off had to plant a message before offering fun. Didi took the mic from Anan and walked onto the centre of the stage. 'Without a slide pack, I feel like a fish taken out of the water, gasping for oxygen.' Some cheerful booing came from the crowd that spurred Didi on. 'But I can offer you something better; a story I've found in the blog of John Romaniello, a writing coach and business mentor frm the Big Apple.

'Look at Marvel's The Avengers, featuring Iron Man, Captain America, the Hulk, and Thor. I haven't got a clue how many of you are hooked on comics, but I bet none of you have paid attention to a great lesson about teamwork The Avengers provide. And not just teamwork – but the value of teams themselves.

'The Avengers' lesson is that one team is not only better than one person but also better than five, ten, or any score of individuals. The key difference is not in the numbers. A group of five can probably accomplish more than one person alone, but it's when those five people work together as a team, the magic happens.

'The hard part is making those five individuals put their egos aside, trust each other, and act as a team. Captain America and Iron Man have a pretty different view of the world, and compromise doesn't come easy. But they respect and trust one another despite their disagreements, and they can see the value the other brings to the team.

'The abandonment of ego is what allows you to become part of a whole that is greater than the sum of its parts. Such a truly cohesive unit that functions with a single purpose can accomplish wonders.

'The Avengers, like any team, is made up of a group of deeply flawed individuals. It is a ragtag crew formed by epic badasses. But their story shows us that, with the right mindset, individuals become a team that can fulfil any objective. Even if it's to save the world.'

Didi paused. The crowd remained quiet and focused. The initial restlessness had given way to introspection. So, Didi pressed on. 'Broadly speaking, our HAHAP team will include over a hundred people, may be more. And there are only three roles involved in making it a cohesive unit, and achieving consilience. I heard that from Chris Hadfield, the Canadian astronaut.

'In *An Astronaut's Guide to Life on Earth*, he suggests that in any new situation, whether it involves an elevator ride or a space expedition, you will almost certainly be viewed in one of three ways. As a minus one: actively harmful, someone who creates problems. Or as a zero: your impact is neutral and doesn't tip the balance one way or the other. Or you'll be seen as a plus one: someone who actively adds value.

'At first, on a new team or in a new situation, every team member's goal should be to avoid being a net-negative contributor. But that's not the end of it.

'If starting from the very outset you look to be a plus one, the veterans will be jealous, and question your claim to fame. Instead, win their confidence and trust by being a zero. This means pulling your weight, humbly showing up, not trying to be in the spotlight, doing your job professionally, asking questions, and learning the ropes. In time, you'll earn people's respect and can move from zero to plus one contributor and someone that others will want to follow. This may be the longer play, but it's far more effective for winning confidence in the long run.

'My project manager's credo is based on Chris's maxim: Don't be a hero, be a zero.'

Crashing applause followed an instant of silence. Didi humbly bowed and climbed down from the stage. On cue, a machine roared up somewhere close. Judging by the sound of the engine, a rather big machine. The engine strained, and a crawler crane with a fair-sized wrecking ball hung from its jib clattered out of its concealment behind the warehouse side wall.

The crowd gasped in bewilderment. The crane, its rattling steel tracks leaving a trail of pulverised oxblood bricks, reached the position in front of the façade and lurched to a stop. The engine revved and the jib swung, sending the wrecking ball in slow motion towards the brickwork. The ball struck with deadly precision, opening a ragged hole in the middle of the façade. The ball swung again, and the part standing to one side of the hole came crashing down in a cloud of dust and debris.

The ball then swung for the third time, to neatly bring down the remnants of the façade. The crane's motor shut down. The operator, wearing a white overall smudged with oil stains and a scratched white hard hat, climbed down from the cabin adopting for a moment a triumphant pose with arms akimbo. Then the figure took off the hardhat, and threw it high in the air. It was Anan!

The crowd erupted in an ovation. A swarm of balloons rose into the blue sky and the klezmer band joined in with a timeless rendering of Abi Gezunt. The fun started.

* * *

The setting sun bathed the warehouse ruin in a warm orange glow. For several hours, the partying had been in full swing. No one had left. Even the board members remained, and not just standing in a secluded group of the Chosen but mixing with line staff, engineers and designers.

But when watery violet dusk fell on the grounds, leaving only the top of warehouse walls and the skeletal roof girders illuminated, Didi noticed a sudden change in the crowd's mood, a strange hushing effect. During a lapse of only few minutes, conversation switched from loudly jovial to shushed and worried. More and more people fell silent, looking at their phones.

This sudden and abrupt change in the crowd's mood caught Didi on the party's periphery. Anan climbed the stage. The music stopped in mid-tune. Anan took the mic and spoke in a calm and controlled voice. 'Many of you have become aware of breaking news. A bloody and violent coup has taken place in Sanriol. Widespread artillery- and gunfire is reported from Zourbagan. Government forces continue offering resistance, but insurgents have gained control of the presidential palace and critical infrastructure objects.

'The fate of the president remains unclear. At the moment, we've got no information regarding the whereabouts of our CEO and the Chief. Cell phone networks have ceased operating.

'Ours has been an excellent feast. But given the circumstances, I guess it's getting time to wind it down.'

* * *

Didi intended to sleep late the next day, but instead woke at dawn and, despite much tossing and turning, couldn't get any more sleep. The news from Sanriol remained vague and conflicting. The only thing everybody seemed to agree on was that the coup had been successful, turning a new page in the twisted history of Sanriol politics.

In the office, the overall mood of solemn contemplation prevailed, aided by skiving caused by the party hangover. Still way before eight, Didi got a message from Anan who, more likely than not, hadn't slept much, being concerned about news from Sanriol. The harbingers of doom hinted at a brusque turn for the worse in the company's future.

'Morning Didi.

Well done with the kick-off meeting. I've never been before to one both so pleasant and effective in achieving its set objectives. Having a barbecue has been a wild idea that I could never have imagined would work so well!

Board members shared this feeling. Several of my colleagues voiced a highly complimentary opinion of the whole process of project initiation, which delighted me no end. HAHAP's colours are flying high indeed, among both executives and line staff. It will make it easier to secure their involvement in project delivery, which in the light of developments in Sanriol has become more important than ever.

Anan

Didi didn't hesitate to place praise where it belonged.

Good morning, Anan,

Thank you so much for your kind words. In fact, the wild idea for the barbecue was Mirai's, whom I'm really happy to have on the project team. Of course, it wouldn't be possible either without the help of Sasha, Azar, Monet, and Kim, and finally, your own involvement and support. Your wrecking ball act will remain in the company annals, I'm sure.

Kind regards,

Didi

A10 - Conduct a focused communication

DIDI DIALLED an extension from memory, inviting Sasha for a chat in the Sky Lounge. Outside, a sudden gust of rain poured in torrents, spattering the panoramic windows with sheets of water. When they settled down with their coffees at one of the free tables inside the lounge, awkward silence descended, and Didi hurried to break it.

'Hi Sasha. We need to follow up on the kick-off with the focused communication. Its purpose is to make sure that everyone in Artophyle is aware of HAHAP objectives and benefits it aims to realise for the company, emphasising HAHAP's link with our corporate culture and identity.

'The focused communication will, inshallah, prevent everyone remaining focused only on their specialist activities, without having a sense of the project as a whole, and without being able to share in and become committed to the overall project goals. That's the only way to nurture proper collaboration.'

Sasha remained silent for a while. 'I'm not sure where I come into the picture.'

Didi couldn't believe it. 'You come from sales and marketing, right? What I have in mind is to do some company-internal marketing. But it still remains marketing, doesn't it, for which you are eminently qualified, right?'

Sasha held the ground. 'I'd say it's more PR than marketing.'

When confronted with evasive mulishness, Didi's fuse tended to considerably shorten. 'Let's not quibble about terms. How do you suggest to market HAHAP launch to Artophyle?'

Sasha must have correctly interpreted the steely notes ringing in Didi's tone and caved in. 'We could put up a big roll-up banner in bold colours with a dynamic slogan, something like "The Halls of Harmony project will take Artophyle to a higher orbit. Our corporate future begins today".'

Didi offered some lukewarm enthusiasm. 'Not bad for a start, but crank it up another notch.'

Sasha got desperate to finish this excruciating improvisation. 'Oh, right, let me think. What would you say if I asked Noor to sketch an artistic rendering of the design and use its outline for the background? We could later use this banner for roadshows, too.'

Didi's tone softened a shade. 'That's more like it. Get it all done as quickly as possible. And last but not least, don't forget to confirm with Elvan from internal services that it is OK to put the banner in the lobby.'

Calming down quickly after the tiff with Sasha, Didi closed project initiation by sending an email to complete Activity A10.

> Hello everyone,
>
> Here is a quick note to let you know that the project's sponsor, Anan, has authorised the launch of the Artophyle Halls of Harmony project. Delivery will start in the next days. You are likely to have a part to play in this project at some stage, and the project team and myself are looking forward to that.
>
> The Halls of Harmony is a convention centre we will build in place of the existing old warehouse at Tea Clipper Wharf. It will first serve as the venue for the quadrennial Save the Planet Award ceremony and later on be used for our own events as well as external ones, predominantly of an artistic and cultural nature.
>
> Our target is to finish this project within 24 months.
>
> Kind regards,
>
> Didi

On the way home in the evening, Didi saw building management handymen hammering in the lobby, assembling mounts for the HAHAP banner.

Monthly Initiation

B01 — Revise and refine the plans

B02 — Have the monthly cycle peer-reviewed

B03 — Make a go/no-go decision

B04 — Kick off the monthly cycle

B05 — Conduct a focused communication

B01- Revise and refine the plans

BIG WAVES that had come hundreds of miles rose to their full intimidating height, before roaring to a foamy crash onto the fist-sized pebbles and waist-high boulders of the Ayakashi Beach. It resembled the Giant's Causeway, but recreated in fluid, rounded forms. In Artopolis lore, it figured as a haunted shore. Even dipping a foot into its waters was fraught with the direst of consequences.

The latter certainly came true, regardless of whether one believed in ghouls in general and yōkai spirits in particular. The waves were high, tide rips treacherous and, most importantly, the water so foul that ingesting even a few drops was likely to result in a lengthy hospital stay.

The port with its industrial excretions lay on the southern shore of the bay, and the mouth of the Dàhé river added to the broth in terms of both foul smell and substance. A bit further out along the north shore, nature prevailed over humans, the water cleared and the yōkai curse weakened. During the sizzling summer weeks, half of the Artopolis population migrated to the Sands.

Didi preferred to pass the time on the Ayakashi beach, which was as scenic, atmospheric and empty as one could wish. The narrow strip of cobbles, rock heads and gravel was squeezed between the sea and the steep cliff that extended for miles. On top of the cliff, high above the perpetual onslaught of the waves, stood some of the more expensive Artopolis real estate. A frayed neckband of fifty to sixty-storey towers of spacious apartments lined the full length of the cliff, serving as a coulisse to another famous promenade, the Bay Boardwalk, that rivalled the Grand Concourse in the splendour of its scenery, splitting city flaneurs into two bands.

Sitting high on a boulder with water surges foaming around it, then ebbing, Didi shifted gaze between the cadence of the waves and a skyscape of cranes beyond the port. The Halls of Harmony were low-slung by design and could not be seen from the sea, being eclipsed by the taller structures lining the waterfront. But the building was there, all right.

Two years had passed since HAHAP had been launched and many of the days in between had become etched in Didi's memory.

* * *

In the week following the Sanriol barbecue, as it went down in the Artophyle lore with the usual dash of healthy sarcasm, Anan called Didi for a chat. Unexpectedly for the latter, they marched several floors up to Eka's cluttered office. Anan brushed away the assistant and kicked in the door.

Eka coldly stared at the impostors above the reading glasses, frowning. Anan remained unfazed by this display of administrative haughtiness. 'Cheers, Eka. Sorry for the intrusion, but I felt it necessary to put us on the same page. Late night yesterday, they found the bodies of Rilke and the Chief. Poor chaps were shot in their car. Riddled with bullets, actually. Such a sad end. Didn't I tell them to get the hell out the moment intel got wind of coup preparations? But the bosses of this world never listen to a humble man. Regardless, those insurgents are real bastards, aren't they?

'Today at five in the morning, Schwartz – the ArtoHolding supremo, in case the name didn't ring a bell - called to congratulate me over with appointment as Rilke's successor. You can spare the applause.'

Eka's chin dropped in the soup. Such an absolute degree of incredulity could not be feigned.

Anan offered the kind smile of a hungry hippo. 'As a consequence, I have to put down my sponsor's role. Or rather, pass it on – to you. Sadly, the Zourbagan financial district project has died while still in the womb. As you'll need something to keep your shop busy, I deliver you to HAHAP. Not quite the same wing span, grant you, but still potentially a fat feather in Artophyle's hat.

'And with that I leave you, my two turtledoves. And to you' Didi, I'll be eternally grateful for giving me the opportunity to get back at the controls of a wrecking-ball crawler. Felt like going through a time warp. Cheers!'

Anan left. Didi stood at ease. Eka took off the glasses, closed eyes and twiddled thumbs for a while, then came back with a sigh and yelled through the closed door. 'Kim, come in, you weasel.' And added, addressing the view behind the window. 'Take a seat, Didi and tell me all I need to know.'

Having been painted into a corner, Eka proved to be a quick learner. It helped that the sponsor's role didn't impose particularly high demands on the incumbent in the first place, being focused on making high-level decision and avoiding getting in the way of the project manager.

In possession of an engineering background, Eka showed an instinctive inclination towards micro-management. But when Didi patiently explained the practical implications of interfering with the day-to-day project management, Eka grudgingly agreed that it would be against everyone's interest. It pleased Didi no end that this key understanding could be reached so quickly.

Having settled that, the rest proved to be a turkey shoot. Rilke's sad fate had given a vigorous shake to the kaleidoscope of power and the shards had rearranged themselves into a very different pattern, converting a major HAHAP spoiler into its ardent champion. Eka's career now as good as depended on HAHAP success. What a twist.

The weather being too good to stay indoors, Didi and Mirai relocated to what they called 'the outer office', a bustling sidewalk café on the flaneurs' mile. Sipping lime and ginger lemonade, Didi kept a serious face, which was befitting for the earnestness of their discussion. 'Our next move is to complete the monthly initiation. And the first activity, B01, is aimed at refining and revising the project delivery plan for the upcoming month.

'Project initiation by intent calls for the creation of high-level plans. Though offering a perfect fit for their purpose, they lack the detail required for the actual project delivery. As a consequence, they need to be revised and detailed one month at a time. Besides, the project operational environment remains inevitably fluid and all plans, including the high-level plan for the whole project, have to be periodically updated to match the ever-changing reality.

'End of lecture in project scheduling 101.'

Didi took a sip of the lemonade and Mirai jumped at the opening. 'Do the cycles have to match calendar months and start at the beginning of the month? Or can they start, for example, on the 20th of each month?'

Didi nodded approvingly. 'Good question. To put it in a nutshell, it's up to us. When multiple projects run in parallel sharing the resources, it may be a good idea to have different cycle starts for them. This way, their monthly initiations do not occur all at the same time. If that's not the case, it comes more naturally to start each cycle at the beginning of the month.'

Mirai arched the eyebrows. 'As the sole focus of our project team is on HAHAP, that'll be our case, right?'

'Right, I think it's best for us to start cycles at the beginning of each month.'

In typical manner, Mirai appeared to go through a mental checklist, ticking off questions one by one. 'So, it's the 18th today. Should we then only aim to plug the gap remaining until the end of this month?'

Didi enjoyed both the ambiance of 'the outer office' and Mirai's meticulous persistence to an equal degree. 'Once again, it's our call to pick our favourite option. When there's more than half a month left, it makes more sense to bridge the gap until the end of the month. And when it's less than half a month, an extended cycle applies that involves planning until the end of the next month. Naturally, there may be variations, but at least that's what the rule of thumb suggests.'

One good way of ensuring that you correctly understood your interlocutor was to summarise or rephrase their statement, then asking to confirm that your rendering was correct.

Mirai had long since mastered this technique. 'So, Didi, that would mean that we start the cycle today, on the 18th of the month, and continue it for forty-two days, until the end of the next month?'

Didi made a slurping sound, chasing the last drops of lemonade with a straw. 'You're spot on Mirai, I think that's a good choice. Ah-h, there's too much sugar in this lemonade, which leaves it not tangy enough by far. Let's get back on the office treadmill. At least, figuratively speaking.'

The first thing Didi did upon returning to the office was to get a bitterly black coffee to wash away the sugary aftertaste that lingered in the mouth. In the meantime, Mirai took the initiative. 'What should we do during this first monthly cycle, then?'

Didi leafed through the deliverables map. 'In accordance with the high-level schedule that you've prepared, we'll be working on site mobilisation, setting up of the Conex container camp, and preparation for warehouse demolition', Didi chuckled, 'giving due thanks to Anan, who has already helped us by doing half of the job at the kick-off meeting. But we'll need to run it past the project team.'

Mirai looked a tad bewildered, if not to say miffed. 'So, Didi, do you mean that we have to ask the team what they want to do during the monthly cycle, and that would be the plan?'

Didi energetically disagreed. 'No, that would kick the legs from under us. Rather, we go by the project schedule but double-check it with the team to make sure it's still realistic. That's the fine line that separates participative management from anarchy. Let's schedule a brief get-together for later today or tomorrow.'

Mirai remained stubbornly unconvinced. 'But how should we go about it?'

Didi sighed, displaying the patience of Job. 'I hereby appoint you a licensed contrarian. Take those high-level deliverables that belong to the upcoming month, break them down into their configuration items and add those details to the schedule. Avoid getting carried away by the detail; too little is bad, but too much can be even worse. Figure out the minimum that'll satisfy the practical needs. And don't forget to double-check for any impacts on the rest of the plan. I suppose you can get it done by tomorrow, can you?'

Mirai nodded. Like most things in P3.express, it didn't look like a very complicated task.

Didi nodded to acknowledge Mirai's nodding. 'Brilliant. It's a handshake deal, then. Tomorrow morning I'll convene the meeting of the project team to review the updated schedule, confirm that they find it realistic and assign the custodian to each work package. Product ownership will highlight accountability.'

Being a scholar of project management, Mirai quickly saw where P3.express work-flows connected to the concepts used in other, more sophisticated, project management methods.

Elements listed in the high-level plan could be viewed as delivery steps, meaning a sequence of work packages that aimed to produce some kind of an interim product. Mirai's current task involved breaking the delivery steps into the actual work packages that could be passed on for execution to custodians and, ultimately, suppliers.

During the years of university studies, doing precisely that had become one of Mirai's favourite occupations. Producing a monthly schedule that included only three delivery steps presented a no-brainer.

* * *

According to Artophyle organisational culture, employees deemed holding meetings on early mornings as inconsiderate and generally bad taste. Work hours often stretched into the night, commuting during the morning rush-hour took an eternity and, accordingly, employee grumpiness rarely dissolved before noon.

Despite keeping highly irregular office hours like everyone else and over and above that and also being among those who lived the furthest from the office, Didi had never really understood this childish proclivity for stomping feet and being generally angry with the world. In Didi's view, being grumpy and short-fused showed more disregard to colleagues than early meetings.

Accordingly, Didi had gradually developed a firm preference for early-morning meetings. Like starting at half seven. Colleagues showed an equal degree of crankiness regardless of whether the meetings started at half seven or half noon. But an early meeting at any rate left more time for the follow-up, that at least in theory paved the way for going home a bit earlier. This last part, though, panned out only rarely.

Mirai radiated goodwill and eagerness. Azar, Monet and Kim looked a bit under the weather, but their general lack of spunkiness remained well within the morning tolerance.

Didi started out on an affable note. 'Good morning. Thank you for making it here on time. The Metro has been rather full today, hasn't it?'

Kim shrugged. 'I've borrowed a velocipede. Artopolis is mostly flatland, so it's no big strain. And traffic this early is just starting to seize up.'

Monet's morning experience looked equally mundane. 'I wish the mayor followed up on the electoral promise and extended the cable-line network. Cable is so much more comfortable than the Metro.'

Azar's creative mindset raised an expectation of out-of-the-box thinking that got fulfilled. 'Oh, you know, I live in Three Oaks, in the artists' colony, and this morning a friend of mine took me for a ride.'

Mirai's eyes widened and everyone else choked on their coffees. 'Do you mean you've been tricked?'

Azar laughed with a child's delight. 'Got you! No, I meant literally, we rode a pair of horses to the city. I found that great fun!'

Didi looked incredulous. 'But you can't do that! Only police horses are allowed in the city!'

Azar shrugged. 'At this hour, I doubt if anyone cares. And besides, my friend serves in the police, and we actually rode police horses!'

After a moment of stunned silence, everyone started hooting with laughter. The mood lightened, chasing off the morning's moodiness. Didi dried the laughing tears and turned to Mirai. 'So, tell us what you've done there.'

Mirai put the schedule up on the screen.

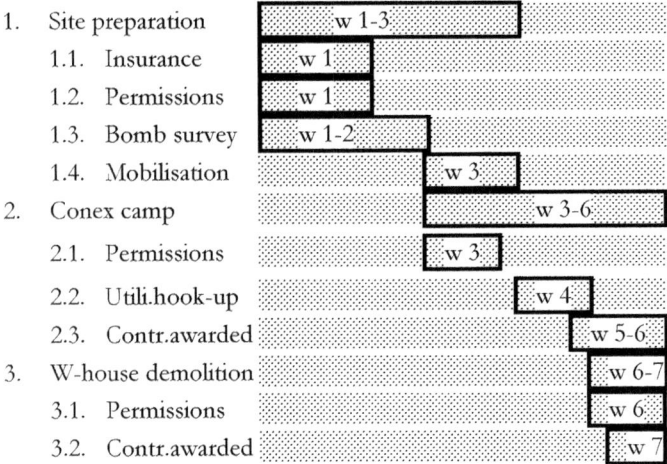

'I find it pretty self-explanatory, actually. As you can see, I suggest changing the title of "site mobilisation" to "site preparation", to also include mobilisation prerequisites like buying insurance and receiving permissions from city authorities.'

Kim's sharp engineer's eye promptly focused on an unusual deliverable. 'And what do you mean by "bomb survey"?'

Mirai's affected an apologetic demeanour. 'It's formally called unexploded ordnance survey. You see, during the Great Patriot War both parties heavily bombed Artopolis. Thousands of bombs had fallen in the port area. I bet there were more than just a few that hadn't exploded. During the past decades, experts screened every construction site for sleeper bombs. And as a matter of fact, every so often one had been unearthed. All in all, well over four dozen.'

Didi saw no reason to hide appreciation for Mirai's thoroughness. 'The more we work together, Mirai, the more your broad-gauge thinking amazes me.

'Did you need to make any changes to the high-level project schedule?'

Mirai flashed a schemer's smile. 'No, I built some slack into it at the time, which has now absorbed the few additional work packages.'

Head bobbing in mock admiration, Didi summed it up. 'I hope I don't sound mawkish, but you have a plotter's mind, Mirai. You know, you seem to defy the old adage saying that the earth was made round so that we would not see too far down the road. Anyway, it seems like we're done with B01.'

B02 - Have the monthly cycle peer-reviewed

DIDI AND MIRAI stayed behind after other team members had left. Mirai looked content. 'Thank you for applying the oil can so generously, Boss; it gave my standing in the team a big boost.'

Didi decided to leave the 'boss' unnoticed. 'You deserved every word of my praise, Mirai. That's the bone truth of it.

Now, let's focus on the job. Next in monthly initiation comes Activity B02 – Have the monthly cycle peer-reviewed. Initially, I thought about asking our star project manager, Tiam, to do the peer review again.

'But one idea behind peer reviews is to have a different reviewer each time, if possible. That'll increase the diversity of opinions and at the same time help share knowledge among a broader range of project managers. For peer reviewers, it can also become a learning experience.

'So, let's try to get hold of Jehan instead.'

True enough, Jehan, like Tiam, enjoyed cult status in the company, though in a rather different way. Jehan had a dry and wiry build, looking as indestructible as an ancient tree root, and as glitzy and mercurial as one, too. Somehow, Didi felt an almost pious reverence whenever approaching Jehan, despite the fact that the latter had a firm reputation of never declining a colleague's request. 'I don't know if it's a good time to ask you this, Jehan, but would you accept to be the peer reviewer for the first monthly initiation of HAHAP?'

Jehan looked at Didi with a calm and piercing seer's gaze. 'It's never a bad time for turning to a colleague in case of need, Didi. Though I admit that my attitude is not fully devoid of a selfish interest. I try to learn with every breath I take, and the way HAHAP has been set up offers me some fascinating insights into the P3.express approach to project management. Take a seat, and let's have a look together, and a chat. That's the best way of seeking the truth. It also tends to be the more enjoyable one and can save time, too.'

Knowing Jehan's character, Didi had prepared for such a productive turn in their conversation. 'Thank you, Jehan, I deeply appreciate your attention and your attitude. Here is the monthly schedule.'

For several minutes, Jehan concentrated on HAHAP documentation. 'Ah, I can see you are using the critical path method for scheduling. True, it's just one of many to choose from, but it happens to also be my favourite.

'Now, there is a rub. You intend to contract external suppliers for the bomb survey, Conex camp and the actual warehouse demolition, right? And as our procurement department will review and sign all such contracts, you'll need to include in the project team its representative.'

Didi's face shifted into a worried frown. 'I thought that I'd sign them myself, as long as they remain within the monthly tolerances approved by Anan, oops, sorry, I meant Eka, the sponsor. After all, the project manager has the authority for the day-to-day running of the project within agreed tolerances.'

Jehan raised a hand to dispel Didi's worries. 'It's not about controlling disbursement. You as the HAHAP project manager remain the master of the monthly budget within the agreed cost tolerance.

'It's rather about the legal implications of entering into contractual agreements with external parties. Such contracts can be sensitive, as given the merest of opportunities, suppliers will never hesitate to try to steal the blanket off you. A simple oversight can cause a lot of trouble for the company.

'In fact, we've had a case recently, where a project manager signed a seemingly simple and straightforward contract for scaffolding. Rather soon after, it turned out that the small print in that contract committed Artophyle to using that company for scaffolding for the next five years!'

Didi raised eyes in genuine despair. 'I didn't realise suppliers could be that tricky and scheming. Is there a place for trust and honesty left in this world?'

Jehan shrugged with a kind smile. 'In your heart, my friend, only in your heart.

'Suppliers' questionable mores are nothing personal; it's just business. Their focus is on their business case, that's all. But that's the reason we have this policy now, that only the procurement department can sign contracts. There are legal experts in that department who make sure it's done properly.'

Here Jehan stopped and pulled at an ear-lobe, focusing the gaze on a spot beyond the distant horizon. 'This upside has a downside, though. A review by the lawyers tends to make the contracting procedure a tad slower, which has to be reflected in the schedule. Just call Zia, who'll be your contact person in the procurement department and ask to check that your schedule is realistic. And don't forget to add Zia to the list of HAHAP stakeholders.'

Didi jotted down notes on a pad. Jehan waited for as long as it took before continuing. 'This will be easy to resolve, at least relatively so. But it raises a somewhat more complicated question. The schedule that we are reviewing only includes contracts for the upcoming month, right?'

Didi nodded, rather clueless regarding Jehan's line of reasoning.

Jehan sighed. 'It's a safe bet then that there'll be plenty more supplier contracts later on in the project. Which means, it'll make good sense to include contract review for each of those as separate work packages. And to schedule those well ahead of the planned contract start date.

'In a nutshell, the schedule for the current month should include contract review for all contracts that are anticipated for the next month. For the review of more complex contracts, a better approach could be to build in a two-month lead. Such rolling planning will win you plenty of kudos from Zia. And what is at least equally important, reduce the plan slippage to acceptable limits.

'Your goal in Activity B01 is not limited to detailing the plan for the upcoming month, but also includes revising the whole high-level project plan as needed.'

Didi shifted awkwardly in the chair, chewing a pencil. 'I admit that we've not thought too much about the other supplier contracts, and didn't reflect them in the schedule. To say nothing about including contract reviews as separate work packages.'

Jehan offered a solemn smile. 'Learning can be painful, but it is akin to the teething pain. A set of new teeth will allow you to chew on larger bites.'

During the whole discussion with Jehan, Mirai stayed quiet, and for all practical purposes, invisible. On the way back to HAHAP control centre – Didi's unassuming desk – the intern finally unzipped the mouth to make a grave observation. 'I can see the need for growing myself a second row of scheduler's teeth.'

Didi chose to offer no reaction to this opening remark, intrigued to hear what would come next. Mirai, however, quickly regrouped, assuming a blasé attitude and going on the offence. 'I'm still too new to Artophyle's ways to anticipate that kind of planning hiccup. And in any case, one thing you learn very early is that the scheduler's job is never done. Even the best battle plan falls apart as soon as the first shot has been fired.

'Doesn't look to me such a big deal. But I'll need to have a chat with Zia to figure out the actual amount of time we need to schedule for. Give me until tomorrow and I'll fix it.'

Once again, Didi felt a nagging doubt. Delegation worked marvels. In principle. But could one get hooked on its pleasures and start abusing it? What if Didi had not delegated the preparation of the monthly schedule? Would that have prevented this glitch? No, not really. The bone truth of it was, Didi had personally reviewed the monthly schedule and not found anything wrong with it. Plain and simple, Didi couldn't shift the blame for the current snag.

This realisation explained why Didi left the office in a less-than-buoyant mood. But melancholy was quickly chased away by the bands along the Grand Concourse, playing morenadas y caporales in rehearsals for the march of the ch'utas called for the next weekend.

Peer reviews - a fundamental element of P3.express – didn't focus on pointing fingers or otherwise pillorying project managers for their mistakes, true or perceived. Rather, they aimed to trigger critical introspection. Beyond discovering and correcting actual mistakes, they helped project managers grow in their jobs.

When Didi arrived in the office next morning, the updated monthly schedule was on the desk. It looked like Mirai shared Didi's profound aversion to hitches of any kind that snagged project delivery and had wasted no time in putting the derailed schedule back on track as quickly as possible.

1.	Site preparation	w 1-5
	1.1. Insurance	w 1
	1.2. Permissions	w 1
	1.3. Contract review	w 2-3
	1.4. Bomb survey	w 3-4

	1.5.	Mobilisation	w 5
2.	Conex camp		w 3-6
	2.1.	Permissions	w 3
	2.2.	Utilities hook-up	w 4
	2.3.	Contract review	w 3-4
	2.4.	Contract awarded	w 5-6
3.	W-house demolit.		w 5-7
	3.1.	Permissions	w 6
	3.2.	Contract review	w 5-6
	3.3.	Contract awarded	w 7
4.	Rolling contr. review		w 6-7
	4.1.	Pit	w 6-7
	4.2.	Foundations pour	w 6-7
	4.3.	Scaffolding	w 6-7

Giving the revised schedule only a cursory glance – Mirai received clear instructions and scheduling fifteen deliverables hardly involved rocket science - Didi forwarded it to Jehan together with a link to the HAHAP health register. The thumbs-up came back in a wink.

B03 - Make a go/no-go decision

THE GOAL OF Activity B03 – asking the sponsor to make a go/no-go decision went beyond mere formality, ensuring that the project remained justifiable as a whole and thus reminding everyone that the project goal rose above the sum of its configuration items.

The decision to authorise the first monthly cycle mostly presented a no-brainer, since little could be expected to have changed since the go decision had been given at the end of project initiation. In the case of HAHAP, however, a change of sponsor had occurred. And the incumbent sponsor could well have a different perception of the project's viability and benefits than their predecessor in the role.

Sometimes, a project would be fully justifiable when evaluated in isolation. But when considered from the perspective of a single portfolio management system that oversaw all the projects in the organisation, it could lose out to other projects that were being delivered or considered.

Following the coup in Sanriol that had taken the financial centre project off the drawing board, HAHAP's justification looked uncontested. But what might Didi know about the deeper ponderings of Artophyle's business strategists?

Once again, forebodings of impending doom overrun Didi. Anan had a comparatively candid character for a senior executive, with this healthy trait being further complemented by clear aversion to micro-management. Anan also enjoyed a reputation for having a gambler's vein, intuitively knowing when to hold 'em and when to fold 'em, which had added extra zest to their dynamic sponsor-project manager teamwork. All in all, Anan had been a no-nonsense sponsor.

In contrast, finding out what made Eka tick posed a challenge. Form Didi's angle, their brief collaboration in the context of HAHAP had been anything but smooth. Though what if Eka now pursued HAHAP objectives with the same fierceness previously reserved for guarding and advancing the department's objectives? On balance, Didi decided to play it dewy-eyed.

'Eka,

We're ready to start the first monthly cycle of HAHAP delivery. It'll continue through the end of next month because we're already past the middle of the current month. After that,

> monthly cycles will start at the beginning of each calendar month.
>
> We've revised the plans and detailed our work for the cycle, which includes site preparation, setting up the container camp, demolition of the old warehouse and the rolling forward review of future supplier contracts. We aim to finish all these deliverables by the end of the cycle. We also made some changes to the rest of the plan - namely, the addition of tasks for the pre-signature review of contracts with external contractors by our procurement department - but that didn't affect the overall project duration or cost.
>
> I attach for ease of reference the deliverables map, product description, high-level plan as well as the monthly schedule. Please let us know about your decision.
>
> Regards,
> Didi

The last phrase bothered Didi, who after some fiddling with words, replaced it with: 'Please confirm that we can start the first monthly cycle.' In days long past, that had been called 'self-fulfilling prophecy'. The current expression was 'affirmative thinking'.

Since no precedents existed for how long it would take Eka to react, Didi went up to the roof cafeteria for a decent meal. The project manager's wisdom insisted on eating and sleeping at every opportunity, since there was no way of knowing when the next opportunity would arise.

As was usual in Artopolis, winter had changed to summery weather with only some ten days of windy and wet spring in between. But the air still stayed pleasantly warm, rather than scorching.

On the way to the Sky Lounge's terrace seating, Didi picked up a bowl of porridge with blackberries, salted caramel chunks and a serving of honey. Didi loved porridge. Their continuing relationship started in the army. Didi had served in a roving unit in the country's contested southern territories, with porridge being the only fare they survived on. Following the morale-raising tradition of their battle-scarred unit, soldiers ate it fortified with a dram of a rather fine single malt.

Didi remembered fondly those days of hardship that reeked of sweat, fear and cordite. Life was reduced to its basic elements – eating, sleeping, fighting. Gruelling marches, fierce firefights. Decisions carried a toll in blood, which had quickly weeded out empty suits among the officers. Idiots and wannabees had had a short life expectancy in combat, which had somehow seemed only fair.

With an effort, Didi stopped the flow of memories. This was not a good time for getting hijacked by the past. A chair scraped while being pulled back, and Mirai dropped into it. 'Hey Didi, that's some mighty nice garb you are wearing today. Didn't know you came up here to the roof once in a while; have never seen you here before. How did you like the revised schedule?'

Mirai's sudden materialisation and the following stream of non sequiturs dragged Didi out of the sepia-tinted reverie feeling annoyed and irritated. Didi had never before experienced Mirai being so perkily bold, well, almost flippant. Didi looked at Mirai through narrowed eyes. 'I'm glad you didn't go as far as asking me if I were enjoying the porridge.'

Mirai giggled. 'Didn't know you got so touchy about your food. Or is it only the porridge that you feel so protective about? C'mon Didi, how did you like the new schedule?'

Definitely, for some reason, Mirai had spun out of control, which suddenly made Didi curious about the why. Mirai's excitement bordered on being, well, high? 'I won't share my porridge with you, you little rascal. But I appreciate your effort at trying to comfort and placate me with this wee smorgasbord.'

Mirai's tray included a plate of fancy-looking canapes and amuse-gueules. Didi plucked one and started chewing, smacking the lips. 'Not bad, not bad. Comes rather nice on top of the porridge. Let me try this other one now, too.' More lip-smacking followed. 'Tasty stuff.

'You show gall to keep pestering me about the updated schedules that you've left on my desk this morning. What's so special about those? Why do you show such eagerness for my praise? You don't need to worry. If there were something seriously wrong with those, I'd have let you know. As long as I don't mention it, you can keep breathing. And eating. If there is anything left when I'm finished, that is. Yum-yum.'

Mirai deflated like a punctured tyre, the bravado of a few minutes ago replaced with a forlorn and nervous look. Didi pretended not to notice, polishing off the few munchies still remaining. Licking fingers as the final chord seemed a teasingly elegant coup de grâce but after some deliberation Didi decided it would be overkill. The terrace filled with the lunch crowd and Didi saw little educational value in hectoring Mirai in public.

Instead, Didi turned down the theatrics. 'Mirai, what bug has bitten you? You definitely behave as if possessed by the evil spirits of our cannibal ancestors.'

Didi's straight face and calm tone presented such a stark contrast to the ridiculous message they conveyed, that Mirai collapsed in bubbling laughter. Didi waited patiently for the fit to pass and, when it showed no sign of abating, kicked Mirai in the shins under the table. 'Mirai, I asked you a question. I find it insulting that you don't answer me.'

For some reason, this stern admonition produced the opposite effect. Tears flowed down Mirai's cheeks, accompanied by some stifled gurgling and convulsive arm-flailing. Didi realised that Mirai could be working up towards a real fit, stood up and made towards the railing at the terrace edge. The roofscape that the other day had looked so depressing against the backdrop of the leaden sky now buoyed Didi's spirits. Row after row of overlapping terracotta-shingled roof ranges stretched under the azure dome, creating a strangely pastoral setting.

Mirai approached, still breathing in gasps, and assumed a precarious balance on the top rung of the railing. 'I'm so-o-o sorry, Didi. That was completely unintended. I just kind of lost control of myself.'

'That I could figure out myself,' retorted Didi icily. 'I hate to repeat myself, but what bit you?'

Mirai flailed the arms once, as if intending to take off and soar into the sky. 'I won. In the mayor's Gordo del Carneval.'

This was the mother of all Artopolis lotteries. Didi looked at Mirai with a grave suspicion. 'And what did you win? A ticket to the moon?'

Drained by laughter, Mirai could only muster a feeble smile. 'Rather better than that. I won two artopools.'

Didi choked on the number. 'Mirai, this is a small fortune. It's like what, half your year's salary?'

Mirai nodded. 'Actually, it's closer to my income for the whole of last year. I joined a team of over 100 players by putting a dime in the common fund, and the team's junta bought a ton of shares in different lots. When I realised how much I had won, I had a fit and went hysterical with joy. That happened two days ago.'

Didi helped Mirai to climb down from the railing. 'Any lesson learned for P3.express flock?'

Mirai got serious. Almost. 'Trust your team blindly with your money and your future and have faith in your collective good luck!'

Didi couldn't help feeling a warm rush. 'Well spoken, Mirai. I believe you've outgrown the role of my punching bag. I hereby promote you to the next position on the career ladder: my personal gofer.'

Mirai's eyes lit up with mischief. 'Hm-m, I'm highly honoured, but don't you think that under the circumstances you may be unable to afford me?'

Didi shook a finger moralistically. 'You've just said it yourself – trust your team blindly with your money and your future. And for you, the team starts with me.'

Didi's phone pinged with an incoming message from Eka. Didi's heart missed a beat.

> Didi, all seems fine to me. Please proceed with the first monthly cycle. Let me know whenever you need a decision from me.
> Eka.

Didi sighed with relief. 'And have faith in your collective good luck! That's the spirit, Mirai. That's the spirit.'

B04 - Kick-off the monthly cycle

ON THEIR elevator ride down to the office, Mirai looked at Didi with an inquiring expression. 'Next on our list will be Activity B04 – monthly kick-off meeting, right? Would you like me to take care of it? Maybe a deep-sea fishing tournament? Or a game of golf?'

Didi answered with a shake of the head. 'Thank you for volunteering, Mirai, but this time I'll take care of it myself. With you wrapped all around me, I feel like I am getting blunted.'

Mirai shrugged and retreated into dreaming about moneys.

Didi had a clear idea regarding how to make the first monthly kick-off meeting a memorable event. Its core purpose was team-building, with ensuring all stakeholders sang from same page of the monthly schedule of deliverables forming a secondary objective. Boring speeches and a lethal slide show would nip the team spirit in the bud. Instead, the occasion called for a moveable feast.

Come the next weekend, the weather played ball. A perfect morning of sunshine and a light breeze offered a solid promise of a flawless day. Well before ten, HAHAP stakeholders assembled at the western terminus of the Jubilee line. The healthy turnout delighted Didi. The project team predictably showed in full force, with Mirai, Sasha, Azar, Monet and Kim all ready for action. Tiam and Jehan conducted Zia's induction into HAHAP rituals. Dressed in non-descript hiking gear, Eka chatted animatedly with fellow directors, Imani and Darci.

Didi filled the lungs with air to bark the marching order when the familiar shiny limo pulled up. Out sprang Anan, energetically waving in joyous greeting. The troupe erupted in applause.

In the north-west of the city, Artopolis tenements gradually yielded space to vacant and abandoned lots, overgrown with pampas grass. The Metro terminus effectively marked the end of the line. A flat steppe stretched ahead with a mountain ridge serving as a distant backdrop, bluish and fuzzy in its remoteness.

Marching along a posted and slightly landscaped path offered no challenges. At that time of the year, the steppe looked its absolute best with lush grasses here and there carpeted in flowering irises, hazel grouse, blue flags, speedwells, violets, gentians and patches of tulips. Generous brushes of blue, purple, sunshine yellow and fierce red created intricate patterns of moving colour.

After a three-hour trek, the marching company reached the oasis formed around a fair-sized lake. Scores of apple trees in full bloom grew along its shore, with the air around them zooming with bees. A low table was decked on a platform with oversized cushions for seats that protruded into the lake. A massive willow overhung it, shielding from the blazing noon sun. The team took places around the table, half-reclined on the cushions in the nomad custom.

Didi stood up, raising a hand to command attention. 'Dear colleagues, I'm deeply grateful to you for having accepted the invitation to come here. We'll follow the ritual of our ancestors and pay tribute to their everlasting culture.'

A gasp was heard, with everyone turning to look at an assortment of big vats that stood on trestles over open log fires. Sturdy attendants stirred what was cooking inside with some kind of flattened bats. A bit to the side stood a battery of charcoal grills, with thin wisps of smoke rising from the fat drippings on white-hot coals.

According to the tradition, the light starters included food prepared from horse meat - kazy, chuchuk and sary-zhyurmö sweetmeats served with balloon flatbread.

Starters gave way to competitions in different traditional disciplines. Anan, rather unexpectedly to many, showed absolute mastery in ambler horse racing. Equally out of the blue, Eka impressed everyone with archery skills. Didi and Azar locked in Kurosh wrestling. While Imani beat everyone in the strategy game of ordo played on a pitch, Darci triumphed in the intellectual boardgame Toguz Korgool. Finally, Sasha and Anan performed a demonstration contest in Er Enish, the athletic horseback wrestling.

In different competitions, allegiances shifted and team members hooted for different champions, which further strengthened the team bonding.

After frolicking for a while in the lake to wash off sweat and dirt, all reassembled at the table, hungry as bears, to finally indulge in the big meal that involved eating a whole sheep.

Zhöeröm, alashak and particularly zhorgom - a polychrome multi-textured braid made from strips of lamb lungs, intestine, stomach and fat - disappeared from the table in no time. The main course proceeded with grilled meats, rounded off by beshbarmak. Little conversation ensued, with food enjoying topmost priority.

Finally, when most members of the HAHAP company had pushed away from the table and reclined on the cushions, drowsy with satiation, a server dressed in traditional garb brought the pièce de résistance of the meal: a dish with a sheep's head cooked whole.

With a deep bow, the server put the dish before Anan. As the bearer of ultimate respect, Anan then received the Kalpak hat and took possession of a heavy knife that rather resembled a short sword.

The sheep's head eating ceremony started, making everyone abuzz with excitement.

For a start, Anan shaved meat fragments from the cheeks, nose bridge and the stump of the neck, cut them into smaller pieces and placed in a large bowl filled with clear soup. The bowl went around the table, with everyone taking a sip and fishing out a piece of meat with the fingers. When the bowl came back having made the full circle, Anan opened the skull with a deft blow of the knife and scooped out the brains into the same bowl. Due to their small quantity and unfirm texture, the bowl set off on its new round with a teaspoon. When the bowl returned, the Artophyle CEO gave a short respectful bow and drained it with all the leftovers.

Anan then proceeded to display the skills of a surgeon in removing the black palate and tongue, handing them over to Noor on an ornamental plate. To Noor! Only then did the gathering became aware of Noor's presence, causing a stir of surprised murmurs.

This convincing demonstration of the senior architect's previously unknown stealth skills looked like an illusionist's act. Hearty applause rewarded Noor's uncanny ability to slip unobserved among the participants in the ceremony and suddenly shed the invisibility cloak to receive the platter.

Anyway, the sheep's palate was intended for the finest lady in the company. Noor accepted the role of the prize's custodian until the final recipient was decided by a beauty pageant. The tongue signified Anan's recognition of the senior architect's eloquence.

Next, Anan dispensed with the ears, presenting them to Imani and Kim – the latter choice generating another round of hushed murmurs – as a sign the CEO would listen to their advice.

And finally, amid absolute silence, Anan dug the two eyes from the head with graceful circular movements of the sword-knife, putting them on a plate delicately decorated in gold. Those were the main prizes, on a par with winning the El Gordo lottery.

Anan cut the first eye in half and presented it to Eka, who showed no emotion and calmly chewed through it, looking Anan straight in the eye. The CEO consumed the second half in the same manner, sealing the new level of their relationship with a delicate hug.

Didi knew full well the meaning of this gesture, which amounted to setting up a direct line of communication between the two, like a hotline between heads of state. That definitely boded well for HAHAP.

In the ceremony's last act, Anan divided the second eye and scanned those present, as if uncertain regarding who merited the honour. Suspense was supposed to be part of the ritual and Anan played the hand well. Finally, the sword-knife pointed at Didi, who felt knees going to jelly. Such a credit dramatically boosted Didi's market value.

With a slightly trembling hand, Didi picked up one half of the greasy eye, almost letting it slip. In the mouth, it felt like a gob of slimy resin. Staring straight ahead at Anan with unseeing eyes, Didi chomped it into manageable chunks and swallowed hard. The eye resisted; for one terrible moment Didi wasn't sure who'd get the upper hand. Then it was over.

Anan gobbled up the second half with a huge grin and gave Didi a bone-crushing bear hug. Applause erupted. Everyone lined up to clap Didi on the shoulder or shake hands. Only Eka stayed on the side-lines, digesting the possible fallout from the influence bestowed upon the HAHAP project manager. It certainly didn't make the sponsor's life any easier.

The company returned to the Metro terminus in a kind of a parking-lot train decorated in the Looney Tunes style. Anan rode ahead on a real horse, relaxed and natural as if born in the saddle.

During the round of goodbyes at the terminus, Eka led Didi a few steps away from the group. 'I know you had reservations about me as the sponsor. Forget those; we'll get along famously.'

* * *

The next work day, the office was abuzz with excitement. It turned out that Mirai, the ubiquitous Mirai, had taken quite a few photos at the kick-off, which were now looping on the information monitors throughout the building. Didi could only stare in silent admiration.

B05 - Conduct a focused communication

AGAINST THIS background, Didi brought the monthly initiation to an end by completing Activity B05 – Conducting a focused communication. While the focused communication after project kick-off catered to the broadest audience, the one in monthly initiation addressed the project team and key, directly-involved stakeholders.

> Hello everyone, thanks for attending the HAHAP monthly kick-off meeting and making it such a memorable event.
>
> During this first monthly cycle we will finish three deliverables: site preparation, setting up the container camp, demolition of the old warehouse, plus conduct a rolling review of contracts for the next monthly cycle.
>
> Thanks for all your help so far. I'm sure that all of us look forward to a great start to the project!
>
> Didi

Weekly Management

C01 — Measure and report performance

C02 — Plan responses for deviations

C03 — Kick off the weekly cycle

C04 — Conduct a focused communication

C01- Measure and report performance

IT'S THE WAY of the world that a low follows a high. The kick-off event had generated a great emotional charge. All that eye-sharing and backslapping with Anan! But after a few days of elation, Didi felt the fog of euphoria thinning with reality setting in. The only salvation lay in ploughing on.

Didi felt an ever-growing admiration for Mirai, who seemed to never experience any doubts. Or at least, show them. 'Didi, isn't it high time we proceeded with the weekly management? You know, the monthly schedule looks pretty tight.'

Faced with this argument, Didi had little choice but start rowing. 'Right you are, Mirai. Let's knock them down one by one. Activity C01 is to measure and report performance. Naturally, there isn't anything we can report yet.'

Mirai looked consumed by doubt. 'It can't be that simple, can it?'

Now it was Didi's turn to hesitate. 'Well, as an option it can. But I don't like it. Instead, let's enhance this opportunity for setting up a routine for the execution of future performance measurement and reporting. A template. A highlight report, basically, that includes use of tolerances, management of key issues, dynamics of the summary risk exposure. Possibly throw in a few selected KPIs, like schedule/cost performance indices or funds/time estimate to complete. What do you think?'

Mirai's doubts thickened. 'What I think is, that if we drag in the KPIs at this level of reporting, we'll be the makers of our own misery. In my humble view, there is hardly a need for such granularity in weekly performance reports. Monthly progress assessments and forecast updating will suffice, I suppose. But otherwise, I agree.

'On a different subject, when should the weekly cycles start? As today's a Tuesday, should we start all weekly cycles on Tuesdays? Or would it instil more order if we start them on Mondays?'

Didi made a dismissing hand gesture. 'We had this conversation about the monthly cycles, remember? For weekly cycles it's the same. We can do as we please, provided there is consistency and a link to higher-level organisational procedures. So, normally, we'd prefer to start all weekly cycles at the beginning of the week. But it can be any other day as well, especially if the project shares resources with other projects and it's more effective to follow a rolling schedule of weekly cycles. Since this is not our case, we can forget about this constraint.

'And for the partial weeks, we can either have a small, partial cycle, or just merge them into the next one.

'The most important thing now is to keep on the move, as otherwise we'll lose momentum, and the project can stall.'

C02 - Plan responses for deviations

MIRAI LOOKED delighted to keep moving. 'Next comes Activity C02 – Plan responses for deviations. As we've just started, there are no deviations yet. But as you say, Didi, it makes sense to use the moment of calm to figure out a routine that will apply in the future.

'Actually, I may have been too quick to shun KPIs. Cost deviations can be calculated from plotting earned value against planned value. And we could also use budget cost of works performed and budget costs of work scheduled curves to calculate time variance.

'It may take a week or so to programme a HAHAP reporting dashboard, but the upside is, it needs to be done only once. Could you ask Eka to get you an introduction to Joey, director of the IT department?'

Didi grumbled, 'How come you manage to always stay one step ahead of me, Mirai? Call the team for the weekly kick-off meeting, will you? That will be Activity C03.'

C03 - Kick off the weekly cycle

MIRAI LOWERED the eyes. 'There is a complication, Boss. The project team has grown to such a size that we won't fit in any meeting room.'

Didi stared in disbelief. 'Is that an attempt at a joke, Mirai? Do you mean that there is no meeting room in the Artophyle building that would fit, what, ten people?'

Mirai shrugged. 'There is none suitable that you can commandeer just by snapping your fingers. We need to book it at least a week in advance.'

Didi sighed with resignation. 'OK, this time it'll be the roof terrace, then. We'll be done by the time the lunch crowd converges on the food. And let's get this sorted once and for all. Please book a passing room for two hours on every Monday morning for the next two years, OK?'

A quarter of an hour later, the scrambled project team assembled on the roof terrace. Didi took off without preamble.

'Right, folks, let's go through the tasks for this week and the next. As today's a Tuesday, we'll treat them as one cycle.

'Accordingly, we'll be working on insurance, permissions, bomb survey contract and mobilisation contract. Plus, dashboard programming, which has come up not half an hour ago. I'll be the custodian for this one and see it through with Joey in the afternoon.

'As I have it here, I'm the custodian for insurance. Azar is the custodian for permissions, and Zia is the custodian for the bomb survey and mobilisation contracts. Since I'm speaking anyway, let me brief you on the insurance angle.

'I've checked with four insurance companies. An issue with all of them is that while we need a clearly defined package, they only sell bundles. In the end, I chose two options from two different companies that cover our requirements and offer good value for money.

'Zia is on the ball now, checking the contract for small print. The biggest risk for someone like me in such a case is to miss something seemingly harmless in the contract that will later on have the potential for causing us a big problem. These are really complicated documents written in Byzantine legalese. I'm not that worried, only because Zia and the colleagues in the procurement department are on the job. We'll have a supplier selected and signed up on time.

'Azar, you are next.'

Azar tapped the tablet. 'I'm the custodian for the permissions task. In order to proceed with old warehouse demolition, we need to get permissions from the city. As during the past two years the city hall had gradually transferred permissions management online, it became much easier and faster. I estimate we'll have the required permissions in another forty-eight hours.'

'Do you see any risks?' enquired Didi.

Azar stayed laconic. 'Can't see any. Short of city hall's internet portal is hijacked for ransom.'

'That's no risk', wryly summarised Didi. 'The city will never cough up money to pay any ransom Cyber criminals are not stupid, they know that attacking the city has no point.

'Mirai, your update on the bomb survey contract, please.'

Mirai offered smiles all around. 'That's a piece of cake. Only one company has got the licence from the city to do such work. It's a joint venture between the military and the mayor's office, set up through proxies. They charge a lot but are efficient. They are also aware of the mayor's own interest in seeing HAHAP through, which makes them less greedy and even more efficient.

'I've passed the standard contract to Zia; it offers pretty little leeway. Basically, it's take it or leave it.'

Zia nodded. 'I checked it with our lawyer and we haven't found any hidden hooks.'

Didi nodded knowingly. 'Money makes this world go around. Do you see any risks?'

Zia gave a head shake. 'As our lawyer and their lawyer happen to play in the same pétanque team, we don't expect any surprises.'

Didi nodded again. 'Good so. Now, what about the mobilisation contract?'

Zia suppressed a yawn. 'Sorry about that. Just feeling a bit sapped. Celes here from the civil engineering department had a look in their records and fished out a passing contractor. I'll be checking it next.'

Didi remained bent on going by the book. 'Any risks?'

'That company did site mobilisation for us before, and it all has worked out just fine. They made no attempt at scheming in the contract.'

Didi scanned the team. 'Any questions, concerns, complaints?'

Celes raised a hand. 'I'm new in the team, so, apologies if I sing from the wrong line. The actual demolition job includes two prerequisites, completing the bomb survey and site mobilisation. I could see there is a very small float built into the schedule. Are we really that sure that both these deliverables will be completed on time?

I'm asking because any delay in completing the old warehouse demolition would stall the whole project.'

Zia looked confident. 'Both contracts stipulate the required duration, and there's a provision for damages if they run late. I'd say we can be reasonably sure that they'll finish on time.'

Celes nodded, fears assuaged. Didi made another scan of the group. 'Right, seems no one else has any comments or questions. Thanks everyone for coming. Stay in touch, and see you all in two Mondays' time.'

C04 - Conduct a focused communication

WHEN EVERYONE had left, Mirai stayed. 'Boss, should I prepare a write-up of what's been discussed and agreed?'

Didi looked chagrined. 'Mirai, would you mind to stop kidding me, please! There is no such role as a project boss. You know, such attempts at making up to me don't tickle my fancy.

'And while I warmly thank you for stepping forward with your offer, I'll take care of Activity C04 – Conducting a focused communication, myself.

'It's the project manager's responsibility to ensure that everyone in the team stays on the same page, regardless of whether they attended a meeting or have been excused. Besides, meeting outcomes need to be recorded for the file and made traceable anyway, to avoid possible misunderstandings and reduce the potential for blame-shifting.'

Mirai left without saying a word but seemingly chuckling behind a hand. With a shake of the head, Didi dismissed Mirai's prodding and cobbled together the focused communication on the hoof before heading back to the office.

> Hi team,
>
> Thanks for coming to the weekly kick-off meeting.
>
> As discussed and agreed, we'll be working on the below deliverables until the end of next week:
>
> - Insurance contract (Custodian Didi, reviewer Zia)
> - Permissions (Custodian Azar)
> - Bomb survey contract (Custodian Mirai, reviewer Zia)
> - Mobilisation contract (Custodian Celes, reviewer Zia)
>
> All deliverables are progressing on time. We haven't identified any new risks on this occasion, but let me know if you come up with any later, or if you encounter any issues.
>
> Cheers,
>
> Didi

Didi felt good. The setting up of the project delivery framework inevitably filled the first days in the project's lifecycle. But once the project rails had been put in place, it started rolling down the tracks and picking up speed.

Daily Management

D01 — Manage risks, issues, and change requests

D02 — Accept completed deliverables

D01- Manage risks, issues and change requests

THE DAILY MANAGEMENT activities block began with Activity D01 – Manage risks, issues and change requests.

Most risks and issues originated at work package or deliverables level. Accordingly, team managers identified and captured most of them in a structured way in the follow-up register. The project manager mostly focused on assessing risk and issue severity and impact, topping up tolerances or thresholds and approving change requests, all of the above within the limits of their delegated authority, as well as escalating exceptions to the sponsor.

P3.express allowed project managers a free choice of risk and issue management procedures. From experience, Didi grew fond of IAPIC (Identify-Assess-Plan-Implement-Communicate) for risk management and CAPDI (Capture-

Assess-Propose-Decide-Implement) for issue management and change control.

Issue and risk custodians had the responsibility for recording progress in the resolution of issues and risk mitigation, using the adopted procedure.

D02 - Accept completed deliverables

THE ONLY OTHER activity included in the daily management involved accepting completed deliverables, included by default in project manager's responsibilities. Only in the case of milestone or critical deliverables did acceptance responsibility pass on to the sponsor.

Didi's own experience clearly showed that having too much work in progress caused difficulties. It tended to waste resources, increase the possibility that deliverables wouldn't be fit for purpose and generally reduce the predictability of project delivery.

Mirai lacked such practical experience, but in its place, had a solid grasp of the underlying concept and generally shared Didi's views. Accordingly, the first monthly schedule followed the predictive approach, with just a few deliverables overlapping, and only partially at that. Instead of working on too many deliverables at the same time, an output would be closed before moving on to the next one. When juggling with too many plates, one could expect more than a few to slip through the fingers and shatter.

Didi also taught Mirai to be equally aware of another seemingly artless trap. While many of the deliverables reached a nearly-complete state rather quickly, final adjustments could stretch on. The programme manager faced the temptation to mark them as complete because most of the work had been done anyway. The remaining bugs, though, inevitably crawled out at the most inappropriate moment, demanding attention from the project manager and threatening to throw back the artificially accelerated project delivery.

Azar passed by Didi's desk on Thursday, to submit for acceptance the first HAHAP deliverable. 'Cheers, Didi, happy to report that we've got the necessary permit from the city. We can begin mobilisation and construction work on the site now.'

Didi looked up from the screen. 'Thank you, Azar, well done. Does the permit have any strings attached?'

Azar smiled ruefully. 'I'm afraid it does. For a start, the permit is valid for twenty-four months only. It's the standard duration, nothing aimed specifically against us. If we're not done by then, we'll have to request an extension, and it doesn't come cheap at one artopool per month.'

Didi stretched and sighed. 'It needs adding to the follow-up register.'

ID: R-005

Cause: HAHAP construction permit is valid for 24 months.

Effect: If we can't finish the project in 24 months, we will have to ask for an extension for the permit.

> **Impact:** The extension will cost one artopool per month.
> **Response:** When making decisions that impact HAHAP duration, we'll need to consider the above cost implication.
> **Custodian:** Didi
> **Status:** open.

Azar patiently stood to the side while Didi captured the risk. 'Didi, looking at how you work with the follow-up register, I wonder whether there were any relevant rules of thumb or good practices that we could adopt? You know, us technical people who have been assigned from their specialist departments to the HAHAP team still have rather vague understanding of how to capture issues and risks correctly.'

Didi looked hesitant for a moment and then made the palms-up gesture. 'I am not sure, really, that it is that scientific. I'm happy to share with you some of my own tips, if that's of any use.

'One, avoid including too much assessment information in the follow-up register. Avoid using shorthand or code, either, unless all team members can understand it. Since it has the upside of saving plenty of time during the project lifecycle, we may consider creating our own shorthand but a bit later on. This is hardly our top priority.

'Two, to ensure that all items are closed properly. It's often a good idea to agree on common thresholds and stick to these when closing items.

'Three, it's essential to avoid adding generic responses that are not action-orientated. Responses should be worded in such a way that the team can implement them, and the custodian, measure the result of the response.

'And four, avoid focusing your time and effort predominantly on doing firefighting to control issues. Rather, pay more attention to risks, as unmanaged risks are a major source of future issues. But that's kind of common sense, isn't it?

'Now, is this the extent of the follow-up that the terms of the building permit require?'

Azar made a namaste gesture accompanied by a disarming smile. 'I'm afraid there is more. Because of our site's proximity to residential areas, we're not allowed to make noise between 6 p.m.to 6 a.m. and at any time on weekends, as well as public holidays.'

Didi glanced up in surprise. 'That sounds contrived. The nearest "residential area" is four blocks away. And in between lie abandoned and decaying developments where the only residents are rats.'

Azar nodded. 'What you say is true but on paper they remain classified as residential areas, and the permit is processed by a machine. The automated procedure saves on the red tape but has a warped view of reality.

'I suppose we could find leads into the mayor's inner circle that could help us with the reclassification. That will take time, though, and the outcome, from today's perspective, is a bit unpredictable, while there are, you know, interests that would prefer to keep things as they are. We need to live with what we've got.'

Didi gave another sigh. 'You're right, of course. Let me add this one to the register as well, albeit as an issue.'

ID: I-003

Cause: HAHAP construction site is adjacent to lots classified in city records as "residential areas".

Effect: Accordingly, the construction permit bans noise-generating work between 6 p.m.to 6 a.m. on weekdays and around the clock on weekends and public holidays.

Impact: It will place constraints on overtime work and affect our ability to compensate for eventual plan slippage.

Response: (1) Avoid plan slippage by all means. (2) Attempt to achieve reclassification of the nearby areas into "abandoned wasteland".

Custodian: Didi.

Status: Open.

Didi's face acquired a stubborn look. 'Right, Azar, we'll have a chat about these restrictions during the next weekly kick-off and try to figure out how to go about them. Regardless, I'm happy to confirm acceptance of Deliverable one-point-two.'

As soon as Azar had left, Mirai, who hovered in a holding pattern in the lounge area, came in for a precipitated landing on the guest chair by Didi's desk. 'What's cooking, Didi? About an hour ago I sent you the contract for the bomb survey cleared by Zia, and what do I get in response? Silence! That's not quite like you.'

Didi felt annoyed at own inefficiency. 'Sorry Mirai, but it's only the Looney Tunes Road Runner who can possibly keep pace with you. I haven't been idling, though, talking to Azar. Any risks or issues in conjunction with the bomb survey contract?'

Mirai proudly puffed the cheeks. 'None whatsoever. It's all greens. Them sappers can start come dawn tomorrow.'

Didi clapped Mirai on the shoulder. 'Kudos to you pal; you've just saved us a whole week! I confirm acceptance of Deliverable one-point-three.'

Mirai blushed, embarrassed by praise. 'I understand that achieving completion of deliverables ahead of schedule can bring us an important advantage. That's quite possible, by the way, as I am consistently building float in HAHAP schedules. So, should we keep nagging custodians to prod them on and finalise deliverables ahead of schedule?'

Didi gave Mirai the best impression of a savant's look. 'You see, my young apprentice, there is a fine line between monitoring, encouragement – what you called prodding and nagging. Since HAHAP runs on weekly cycles that are relatively short, it makes sense to let the custodians work during the week at their own pace. In my view, the weekly gateways provide adequate control points.

'At the same time, I'll be actively encouraging work package custodians to report eventual snags and issues that could lead to delays in the acceptance of deliverables as early as possible, preferably before such delays actually do occur. This education will take time and demand a bit of persistence on my part. In many cases, people will intuitively attempt to hide flaws in their work until the last possible moment.

'The best remedy I know is to give custodians of deliverables a carrot for proactive reporting of possible delays bundled with exoneration from punishment for their inability to deliver on time, regardless of its cause. And as another option, conduct a public whipping of those who choose to wait until the deadline was on them to admit they were lagging.

'It takes time to sink in that a carrot is a better reward than a whip, and an admission that you are facing a problem does not imply a loss of honour. But that'll be HAHAP team culture, and trust me, Mirai, we'll get there. I have spoken.'

* * *

Two weeks into HAHAP delivery, the project team functioned as well as Didi could have hoped. They led the monthly schedule by a few days, which was marvellous. It gave the team a most valuable prize: confidence that they followed realistic plans and the team's collective performance was at par.

One sunny mid-week morning, Didi whistled a popular tune under the breath while conducting the periodic clean-up of the follow-up register. Mirai erupted onto the floor like a ball lightning, crackling with pent-up energy that threatened to explode at the merest atmospheric oscillation. Looking at the approaching Mirai's plate-sized eyes, Didi realised at once that something had gone fundamentally wrong.

Reaching Didi, Mirai bent down and hoarsely whispered in Didi's ear. 'They found one. The bomb squad. The bomb. The bomb squad has found a bomb. A big one. A really, really big one. I mean, the biggest that has ever been found.'

Didi was surprised by experiencing absolutely zero panic and, on top of that, knowing precisely what to do first.

Situations that threatened the completion of the monthly cycle within agreed tolerance demanded immediate notification of the sponsor. Didi dialled Eka's mobile number, triggering the sheep's eye protocol.

'Eka, it's Didi. Sorry for the interruption, but we're in an emergency. The bomb squad has located an unexploded piece of ordnance on the HAHAP site. Mirai and myself are going down to the Tea Clipper Wharf to scout the sitch out.'

Eka's reaction was predictably laconic. 'Oh, shoot.'

Next, Didi captured the new issue in the follow-up register.

ID: I-004

Cause: The bomb survey squad has located an unexploded piece of ordnance on the HAHAP site.

Effect: All work on the site halted until further notice.

Impact: Weekly schedule to be reviewed, knock-on implications on the monthly schedule and the high-level project plan respectively as good as certain and very likely.

Response: Monitor the situation, update issue records on a daily basis, update work plans according to situation.

Custodian: Didi.

Status: Open.

The initial response thus required monitoring the situation. On the way out, Didi and Mirai grabbed hard hats and blaze orange jackets with luminescent striping that crews routinely used for visits to construction sites. They managed to get only as far as the Concorde Metro station. There, police had cordoned off all streets leading in the general direction of the Dockland Marshes.

As an immediate consequence, a thick soup made of scores of people and hundreds of stranded tuctucs slowly sloshed between the station and the police tape, getting denser by the minute.

The situation called for improvisation, and Didi was rather good at it. Mirai in tow, they approached an idling cargo tuctuc, explained their requirement and hopped into the cargo bay. The driver pushed through the crowds like an icebreaker through ice slush. At one of the nearby storage huts maintained by vendors to supply their station stalls, the driver piled the cargo bay high with discarded cardboard boxes and jute sacks.

On top went five-gallon flagons of "spring water" used for cooking and washing-up. For these, Didi had to pay, but the agreed price offered adequate value for money.

They then drove a bit further south down the main drag and turned left following the southern boundary of the taped-off Dockland Marshes. There, traffic and people moved along the tape at the usual pace with nobody displaying an intention of crossing over – or, rather, under – into the Docklands. Accordingly, only a few police checkpoints monitored the tape perimeter, posted far apart and with a laid-back attitude to their duties.

When a speeding tuctuc, its front wheel almost riding on air, dashed for the gap in the access control barrier beeping for attention, the police officer lounging in a cruiser waved it through without even leaving the car. A blast wave would offer a safer ride for the two wretched dudes in hard hats and dirtied construction workers' garb who pathetically clung to a Matterhorn of water flagons rising from the cargo bay.

Inside the taped perimeter, life went on as usual. In effect, the Dockside Marshes were pretty much devoid of any life. At least until they got to the second cordon, positioned just off the Tea Clipper Wharf. Some movement could be observed as different pieces of machinery took up their positions. The partial ruin of the old warehouse rose among the rooftops of the decaying squat brownstones that dated back to the times when Calico Jack's crew caroused in the dockland's saloons.

A boost in water supplies actually pleased the bomb busters who manned this second cordon. Under the glaring sun, they unloaded the tuctuc in no time, then let it roll free.

Didi quickly located the site manager, dressed in faded army fatigues sporting a similarly faded name patch that said something like "Olly", or may be "Olay".

Having dispensed with introductions, Didi went straight for the jugular. 'Chief, what's the score?'

Olly looked at the two impostors with uncamouflaged resentment. 'There is something underground that has triggered both sweeper and sniffer alerts. So, it's made of metal and is rigged with explosives. My bet would be it's either Amatol or Trialen, though Octol is always a possibility. And it's big; about half the size of a semi.'

While Mirai just gawked with excitement, Didi pressed on with the questioning. 'What's the plan, then?'

Olly shrugged. 'I dunno. Making plans is above my paygrade. Some bigwig will take over. Run more scans. Map depth and position. Determine the device and fuse type. Figure out how much blasting power it has. Things like that. Then think. But first, evacuate the locals.'

Didi got impatient. 'So, how long will it take to get the site cleared for business?'

Olly shrugged. 'I guess they'll try to get it done before the winter. When the ground freezes, you can't keep on digging. Becomes too dangerous.'

Didi made no effort at hiding abject incredulity. 'Winter? You must be kidding!'

Olly gave a head shake. 'No kidding. No way of telling how it'll pan out. You guys better get out of here, and pronto. With sleepers, you never know what's on their mind.'

Didi sat on the platform of a military-issue flatbed truck, hard hat off, eyes closed and face turned to the sun. Mirai approached, crunching on the grit. 'Looks bleak for HAHAP, doesn't it?'

Didi answered with eyes shut. 'It does. If it were a week or two, we could possibly catch up. The cost will go through the roof but it'll buy us fair odds of finishing on time. If we're stuck for longer, we won't have a snowball's chance in hell, regardless of how much money we'll burn.'

Didi felt like a newspaper sheet that after lying in the gutter for a week had become crumpled, bleached and soiled. It looked very much like the end for HAHAP.

Being unable to think of anything that could be done about it, at least not at the moment, Didi jumped off the flatbed, fastening the strap of the hard hat. 'Let's go, Mirai. We'll have to walk at least half of the way back to Concorde.'

The grinding sound of snapping metal preceded a heavy thump of something crashing down, making the ground shake. Yelling and angry shouting followed. The visible rafters of the old warehouse shook, swayed and started collapsing as if in slow motion. Didi grabbed the frozen Mirai by the hand, dragging them into a passage under a century-old brownstone leading to the inner yard. Didi acted on a hunch and without giving a thought to the potential risks involved in seeking refuge under a decrepit-looking structure. But it came out all right. Mostly.

Pushing Mirai deeper into the passage, Didi, with a stretch of the neck, glanced out to absorb what was going on. A thin cloud of dust rose slowly in the sky. After a moment, the ground shook violently in a scarily profound way. A rumbling kaboom of a sound blast hit Didi like a train. In the following silence, an oxblood-coloured curtain of grit, earth and broken brick rose high above the rooftops.

An instant later, a second tremor shot through the ground, making the brownstone shake and wobble in its foundations. This time, a geyser of ochre-coloured rubble shot up in the air, looking like a foamy jet of cola spraying sky-high from a well-shaken bottle. Didi splayed face down on the potted street, knees having given way without warning.

Debris began falling down in a steady downpour of stone and steel. A fragment hit Didi on the hard hat, another clipped the shoulder. Mirai grabbed Didi's leg and pulled. A cheek grating on the grit was Didi's last memory.

* * *

Didi woke up on a hospital bed from a splitting headache multiplied by ringing in the ears. Mirai's concerned face swam into vision. Didi gave a shaky thumbs-up. Mirai's grimace morphed into a cheerful smile. 'Welcome back to the land of the living! Can you hear me speak?'

Didi gave a tiny nod, careful not to provoke the headache's wrath. Sounds came through muffled but audible. 'What happened? Am I still in one piece?'

With a roll of the eyes, Mirai replied, relieved. 'Oh, no worries, you'll be fine. Looking at the upside, the project is firmly back on track. As a matter of fact, we're leading the schedule by about five weeks now.

'For some reason, a sensor mast on the site collapsed and banged against the wall of the old warehouse, setting off a domino effect. The pummelling received from Anan at the barbecue party had weakened the building's structure and it became unstable.

'The warehouse hitting the ground produced a tremor that triggered the bomb. Its blast caused another shake that triggered the second sleeper bomb close by, which until then had remained undetected. Here is where you got hit on the head by an airborne piece of cement foundation that weighed like half a ton. The brownstone under which we were hiding as good as collapsed, but for some odd reason, the ceiling of the passageway held.

'Your crushed hard hat is now on exhibit in the Artophyle vestibule lobby, making people wonder how come it contains no shreds of hairy scalp or brain matter. Some colleagues feel cheated.'

Mirai roared from sheer delight, doubling up with laughter and almost collapsing on the linoleum floor. Didi didn't join in, finding the sketched tableau lacking in both good taste and elegance of plot. 'If I understand you correctly, Mirai, those chain explosions have made the demolition contract superfluous, right?'

Mirai looked at Didi with admiration. 'You've chosen a very nice way of putting it. But that's not the whole catch of the day. We've also got the pit for the HAHAP foundations made ready in an instant and for free. And on top of that, building stumps within three blocks of the site instantly turned into mounds of rubble, as if touched by the magic wand. The city will now have little choice but to recognise that the HAHAP site is in fact surrounded by wasteland rather than "residential areas". In consequence, we've already applied for dropping all noise abatement restrictions from the construction permit. Not bad, eh?'

Didi grinned from ear to ear despite a sting of pain. 'That's unbelievable! All our risks and issues have been in an instant swiped off the board. Wow, that was some roll of the dice.'

Mirai dried the laughter tears. 'What can I say, pal? That's life, eh? Now, just pick yourself up and get back in the race.'

Which was precisely what Didi did, in time for signing off on the first weekly report prepared by Mirai.

Weekly progress report #1

Planned progress: 0.8%

Actual progress: 3.6%

Forecasts:

Duration → on schedule

Cost → 1,200 artopools (including tolerance); - 32 artopools (savings)

Finished Deliverables:

1.1.   Insurance

1.2.   Permissions

   1.3-1.4   Bomb survey contract reviewed, awarded and executed (lead two weeks)

   1.5.   Mobilisation contract reviewed and awarded

   3.1.   Old warehouse demolition executed (tasks for permissions, contract review, contract award, contract execution superseded) (lead 7 weeks)

   4.1.   Pit completed in rough (tasks for contract review and contract award superseded) (lead 11 weeks)

Closed risks: R-003; R-004;

Open risks: R-001 (custodian Eka); R-002 (custodian Azar), R-005 (custodian Didi)

Closed issues: I-001; I-002; I-003; I-004

Open issues: None

Didi felt relieved and content. 'HAHAP started being at odds with the whole environment around it that has seemingly conspired to block its scheduled progress. But we managed to blast our way through, pardon the pun, and now it'll be smooth sailing for a while. It's important, though, that we don't simply sit and enjoy the ride with the hands crossed. We are leading the schedule, and let's try and maintain this lead.'

Mirai looked a bit hesitant. 'Why don't we exploit the fanfare around how HAHAP, as you put it so aptly, blasted its way through? That has become part of the corporate lore anyway, along with Anan's wrecking-ball swinging feat.'

Didi laughed happily. 'I'm delighted that some events associated with HAHAP have made it into the Artophyle annals. But let's keep project reporting focused on facts rather than circumstances.

'Regarding the report, please circulate it to those stakeholders who are supposed to receive it. We've probably marked them as such in the project description, haven't we?'

Mirai reluctantly dropped the topic of lore and annals, returning to the reality that, in comparison, looked drab and boring. 'Sure, there's a column in front of the stakeholders' names that shows who's supposed to receive the report. Later on, I'll draft a more complete communications management approach. It'll describe who produces what reports and when, and who and how receives them."

Didi nodded approvingly. 'Good. Don't forget to ask report recipients for feedback after a few days, to make sure that the report format and the degree of detail it provides works for them.'

Mirai pinched an earlobe in thought. 'Should I do it then every week?'

Didi gave a head shake. 'It'll feel contrived to ask their feedback each and every week, especially when the format of the report won't change. We'll do it once now in the beginning, and then maybe every couple of months or so to ensure it keeps matching their current needs.'

Monthly Closure

E01 — Evaluate stakeholder satisfaction

E02 — Capture lessons and plan for improvements

E03 — Conduct a focused communication

E01 - Evaluate stakeholder satisfaction

WHEN ONE KEEPS BUSY, time flies. Monthly closure came upon Didi in the blink of an eye. It began with Activity E01 – Evaluate stakeholder satisfaction.

Didi opened the corresponding folder in the HAHAP directory on the dedicated cloud server assigned to Artophyle. Questionnaire forms for assessing stakeholder satisfaction had been finalised ahead of the occasion. One set addressed project team members and, the other, stakeholders external to the team. Both sets produced unattributable data.

Didi pushed the button, and out they went to preconfigured blocks of email addresses.

Didi had set the deadline for returning the filled-out questionnaires in twenty-four hours. Experience indicated that the length of the deadline had an inverse relationship to the number of received responses. This time the return rate clocked at 98% for project team members and 73% for external stakeholders.

Not really a bad showing but still something to work on. Executives, in particular, tended to treat assessment questionnaires with disdain and had to be convinced to take them seriously.

The responses went straight to the health register, meaning that Didi saw only collated results rather than individual answers, supporting stakeholders' trust in the anonymity of the evaluation.

E02 - Capturing lessons and planning for responses

QUESTIONNAIRES HAD the aim of providing baseline information for Activity E02 - Capturing lessons and planning for responses

To look at the results and discuss improvements, Didi called a project team meeting later that same day. This format helped to increase team members' buy-in, plus the Wisdom of Crowds could help in finding optimal actions for areas that required improvement.

Team members

- 92% found it easy to interact with other team members
- 92% found it easy to interact with the project team
- 87% found it easy to interact with external stakeholders
- 94% found their roles and responsibilities to be clear enough
- 81% had a clear vision of the project
- 87% found the project goals realistic

- 87% were happy with the project management system
- 92% were happy with their job overall

Stakeholders external to the project team
- 82% had a clear understanding of what happens in the project
- 77% found it easy to communicate with the project team
- 87% found the project management process clear enough
- 87% found the project to be moving in the desired direction
- 89% were satisfied with theproject so far overall

Didi studied reactions that registered on the faces of project team members. The prevailing attitude showed satisfaction, and no one appeared to be surprised, pleasantly or otherwise.

Didi didn't like this complacency, or possible indifference, at all. 'Look, in broad brush, the numbers look OK. But if you dig just a weeny bit deeper, there are two areas that make me worry.

'First, a full quarter of you still lack a clear vision of the project. Not that I can really fault you. We are only one month into delivery, and I fully realise some of you have joined the team only recently. Accordingly, during the next days, I'll be talking to each of you individually to ensure that you fully understand where this project is going.'

Didi heard an approving murmur and saw a wave of head-bobbing. 'The other situation gives me more reasons to worry. Stakeholders outside our team – many of whom are senior executives – don't find it easy to communicate with us. While this perception is not completely new to me, it requires attention and corrective action regardless.

'Let's apply the Delphi technique that includes five steps: collect ideas; present them as a list to participants; have another round of collecting ideas; review the ideas discussing their pros and cons; vote to decide on the preferred course of action.'

After going through several iterations of the proposed ideas that involved rephrasing, clustering and weeding out, Didi put the final shortlist to a secret ballot, imitating a prolonged drumbeat. 'And the winner is … to use non-technical language in our communications with stakeholders outside the team!'

E03 - Conduct a focused communication

NOW DIDI COULD wrap up the monthly closure by completing the last remaining Activity E03 – Conduct a focused communication, addressing it to all team members to summarise project achievements during the month and thank them for their contributions.

First and foremost, the focused communication in P3.express placed a strong emphasis on the reporting of achieved results, rather than on project promotion.

The focused communication also aimed to remind everyone to keep their sights on the broader project objectives, rather than on isolated, specialised activities, which helped to glue the team together.

Didi knew the ropes: focus on achievements rather than the amount of work done; keep the message clear and avoid corporate talk; keep it short, preferably limited to just a few lines.

> Dear team members,
>
> Thanks to your efforts, and a bit of providential help, we were able to finish these deliverables in the first month of HAHAP execution:
>
> - Site preparation, including insurance, permissions, bomb survey contract reviewed, awarded and executed, mobilisation;
>
> - Container camp set up, including permissions, utilities hook-up, contract reviewed, awarded and executed;
>
> - Old warehouse demolished (with no effort of ours);
>
> - Contracts for activities during the next monthly cycle reviewed and ready for awarding, including pouring foundation, scaffolding.
>
> - Pit preparation (scheduled for monthly cycle #2) completed in the rough (through intervention of force majeure).
>
> Following an assessment of stakeholder satisfaction, we agreed that using non-technical language will help improve communications with external stakeholders.
>
> We'll get together soon to initiate another monthly cycle. Looking forward to talking to you then!
>
> Cheers,
>
> Didi

* * *

An immense wave silently rose and then crashed on the beach with a sound reminiscent of the blast that had put down the old warehouse, startling Didi from the flow of memories. Two years had passed but it felt like it was yesterday. The spray drizzled Didi, water foaming just inches below the top of the rock where Didi perched.

It was almost time to go back to the city, but not quite. Until the low tide came, Didi remained prisoner of the sea, with the rock jutting out of the surrounding water.

This refreshing reminder of the power of the elements fast-forwarded Didi's reminiscences to project closure.

Project Closure

F01 — Hand over the product

F02 — Evaluate stakeholder satisfaction

F03 — Have the closing activity group peer-reviewed

F04 — Archive the project documents

F05 — Celebrate!

F06 — Conduct a focused communication

F01- Hand over the product

TOWARDS THE project end, delivery became a race against the clock. There had been ups and downs, but most of the deviations from the project plan could be compensated by drafting additional workforce or paying overtime. That had naturally driven up the cost, so that Anan had to top up breaches of project cost tolerances on several occasions.

The Artophyle CEO had never considered the premature project closure as a realistic alternative. Once the desired project product had been produced, cost overruns could be presented as a write-off item on the income statement, reducing tax liability and set off by the promise of future revenues. In for a penny, in for a pound. Or artopool, as was the case.

In comparison, the sunk cost produced by the premature closure would cause a black eye to Anan, to say nothing of the gaping hole that failure to host the Save the Planet Awards ceremony would blast in Artophyle's exposure enhancement strategy.

So, the only remaining enemy – but a formidable one - was time. Winning that battle had exacted a heavy toll. But all was well that ended well. Nine weeks before celebrities would walk the red carpet at the inauguration of the Save the Planet Awards ceremony, Didi started project closure.

Activity F01 focused on project product acceptance and handover. Accordingly, Didi had formally requested Eka to designate the owner for the project deliverable. It took the sponsor several days to get it sorted with the Artophyle board, but finally Kyung had been appointed CEO's proxy. That qualified Kyung for inclusion among the project stakeholders.

The updating of the stakeholders list at that – late – stage in project delivery still made perfect sense. The project product might have been completed, but the project only finished after it had been closed.

Kyung, one of the Artophyle dinosaurs, had been a permanent fixture of the executive offices for longer than anyone could remember. A survivor of numerous board wars and a successor to a plethora of perished or banned board members, Kyung affected a comforting presence and a nonchalant attitude to all things mortal. Underneath this disguise lurked a pitiless office predator. Most Artophyle employees feared Kyung like a demon.

While Didi didn't share such strong feelings towards Kyung, the very name sent shivers down the spine. But demon or not, project business had to be transacted to the end. 'Hello Kyung, I am told you'll be leading the hand-over of the HAHAP final output. How would you like to go about it?'

Kyung's voice on the phone sounded warm, almost affectionate. 'My dear Didi, I have heard so much about your exploits on this project. I'm delighted and grateful for having been chosen for this role. I'm sure it'll be a new highlight of my career. Could I prevail on you to come up to my office later this afternoon, say at half three, if it's not asking too much?'

Didi decided to keep a neutral air. 'Of course, Kyung. Your wish is my command.'

Kyung sounded all smiles. 'That's the spirit, dear Didi, that's the spirit.'

Didi wiped the cold sweat off the brow and went to have a coffee with a sticky pudding as a reward for selfless bravery.

At half three on the dot, an assistant ushered Didi into the demon's lair. Kyung rose in a greeting. 'Didi, so good of you to offer me your valuable time. Here is our hand-over team – Ikrimah, Skylar, Guang and Nyoka. They all come from the mayor's office. I'm sure you're aware that our mayor is an important stakeholder and a contributor to this project.

'I suggest they'll go through project records, and after that we'll work on-site.'

Didi put the project folder on the mahogany conference table. 'You'll find her the project description, deliverables map and the updated project plan. If you require any further details, just let me know.'

Skylar had a piercing, cold stare. 'We are more interested in the product functionality than in the paperwork.'

Kyung picked up the thread. 'Absolutely, the project documentation is only the reference point, our north, so to speak. We plan to complete the hand-over in five days. You'll hear from me when we're ready.'

In the end, the hand-over turned out to be almost painless. The mayor's team came up with a list of follow-up tasks that stretched half a mile long. But eight weeks before the award ceremony, that was the least of Didi's cares. Under the circumstances, no one had the intention of delaying project closure through nit-picking. Kyung and the mayor's pack were in the same boat with Eka and Anan. After the dust from the award ceremony settled, Artophyle's maintenance team would take care of the list to mayor's fullest satisfaction.

And then came the grand moment when Kyung delivered the verdict. 'Dear colleagues, as unanimously agreed, I confirm acceptance and handover of the final product of the HAHAP project.'

Didi almost expected champagne to be served, but none came.

F02 - Evaluate stakeholder satisfaction

THIS ACTIVITY presented no new challenges, as it involved evaluating stakeholder satisfaction one last time and, yes, producing the last list of follow-on recommendations. It stood to reason that at that juncture, no particular action could be taken to improve stakeholder satisfaction. The whole purpose of final evaluation focused on building a bridge into the future.

Stakeholder perceptions could become very useful in the formulation of future projects. And even more so when complemented by follow-up actions, as these would make them immediately actionable.

The follow-up recommendations were of the closed kind, meaning that the project manager would analyse and archive them without taking any action. People often called them lessons learned.

F03 - Have the closing activity group peer reviewed

TO CONDUCT the peer reviews during the HAHAP lifecycle, Didi had harnessed the services of all Artophyle project managers. As it looked appropriate to close the circle, Didi called Tiam. 'Cheers Tiam. Could I twist your rubber arm and ask you to do the final peer review of HAHAP?'

Tiam sounded offended. 'You surprise me no end, Didi. I'd be gravely offended if you bestowed this honour on anyone else. Only a giant of my stature would be fit for the job.'

Didi laughed, relieved. 'I knew I stood on the shoulders of giants.'

Tiam offered only one piece of advice. 'Keep buggering Kyung until you receive a formal notification of hand-over and acceptance of the final project product. Kyung is an old sly fox and has a mile-long record of playing little dirty games. So, squeeze the slippery brat until you've got it black on white.'

F04 - Archive the project documentation

STORING AWAY the documentation, on the contrary, presented no challenges. Didi summoned Mirai. 'I've archived all the project documents in the project directory on Artophyle's dedicated server. It has a proper backup system in place, so the archive won't be lost.

'From tomorrow on, it's read-only and only the sysadmin has write access to it. But even the read access will be authorised on a need-to-know basis in accordance with the list drawn up by Eka. So, if any one becomes interested, they need to first be vetted to get on the list and then obtain a separate permission for actually accessing the documents.'

Mirai shrugged. 'All this secrecy looks a bit overblown to me. Why should we be so hush-hush?'

Didi raised a finger in a gesture of admonition. 'Because given a minute's indiscretion, the competition would not hesitate to steal our secrets. Look at it this way. Project files include the detailed description how Artophyle, one, implemented a project that involved major innovation, two, overcame all the issues and three, what it learned in the process. This is valuable stuff.'

Mirai's eyes flashed with naughtiness. 'Given half a chance, will we similarly engage in the stealing of our competitors' secrets?'

Didi again wagged a finger. 'Mirai, you need to understand the difference between competitors spying on you and you using creative methods to acquire business intelligence about competitors.'

Mirai chose not to continue pursuing that thread, switching back to the original subject of their conversation. 'What should I do if later on I find that an odd document has been overlooked and needs uploading to the directory? I won't have write access anymore.'

Didi shrugged it off. 'Sure, it happens all the time. HAHAP has produced a full gazillion of management products. You can always send it to Fede, the sysadmin, with instructions on where to store it. And speaking of it, ask Fede to add the HAHAP directory link to the index of completed projects.'

F05 - Celebrate!

DUSK STARTED gathering. The first stars lit up the dome of the sky. Across the bay, a battery of powerful searchlights projected a barrier of light, revealing the exact location of the Halls of Harmony. Media choppers jostled for the best positions above the venue of Save the Planet Awards ceremony, an event that would be broadcast and streamed globally.

Low tide had come in, making for an easy return to the beach. Didi headed to the foot of the cliff and began the arduous climb to the city.

* * *

The after-event party expectedly turned out on a mega scale. In recognition of their role, Anan had secured for all members of the project mean full-access passes to a dozen or so spin-off events. The music boomed, the strobe lights flashed and the glitzy crowds swayed in the absolute best of moods.

In the middle in the party throb, Didi grabbed Mirai by the elbow. 'Let's have a chat! I have a piece of breaking news for you!'

Mirai made round eyes. With Mirai firmly in tow, Didi struggled through the pulsing throng to a quieter corner of the gardens. Needless to say, Didi knew precisely the spot where the hall's acoustics provided a bit of respite for the ears. 'Before the party started, I had a brief conversation with Anan, praising your talents to the sky. Now don't get shy; you've deserved it. To make the long story short, there's a job offer waiting if you're interested in joining Artophyle after finishing your degree.'

Mirai impulsively hugged Didi, eyes shining with emotion. 'Oh, Didi, this is the best reward I could hope for! Thank you very much indeed! I've got only the final semester left in my studies and I'd love to join Artophyle right after graduation.'

Mirai's hot embrace made sweat break out on Didi's brow and back, making the occasion even more memorable for both. 'Then I'll see you around! Now look up!'

Right above them, a swarm of drones was going through a lightshow. To Mirai's utmost bewilderment, they assembled into a glittering message that filled half the sky:

> 'Mirai, welcome to Artophyle!'

Mirai laughed out in sheer delight and they dove back into the partying, just as the fireworks started erupting in the sky, which had a Martian hue from the city lights.

F06 - Conduct a focused communication

AFTER THE MIND-BLOWING experience of the award ceremony rave, getting back behind the office desk felt like an anti-climax. But Didi had to attend to the final project manager's chore.

The focused communication in project closure had the dual purpose of showing appreciation for the team members and encouraging them for future projects, as well as making the organisation aware of the project results and benefits and its contribution to the achievement of the broader organisational objectives.

Conducting a focused communication at the end of project closure was the responsibility of the sponsor, not the project manager. Didi only had to alert Eka to this requirement. The HAHAP sponsor hardly needed any hand-holding, being perfectly capable of producing a touching communication rather than getting inspiration from drafts prepared by underlings.

> Hello everyone,
>
> Twenty-six months ago, to the day, we took the strategic decision to build a ground-breaking convention centre that could facilitate artistic and cultural initiatives in Artopolis while also raising the public visibility of Artophyle.
>
> Today, the idea became reality, and I'm delighted to say, it's been done very well. I'd especially like to thank Didi, the project manager, for facilitating the whole process and making it easy for everyone to work on this project; to Anan and the rest of the board for supporting us; to Imani, Noor, Azar, and everyone else in the design department for their monumental work; to Kim, Darci, Monet, Zia, Celes, Mirai, and everyone else who contributed. I'm really proud of you all.
>
> Regards,
> Eka

Post-Project Management

G01 — Evaluate the benefits

G02 — Generate new ideas

G03 — Conduct a focused communication

G01- Evaluate the benefits

AFTER THREE MONTHS, the dust blown sky-high by the Halls of Harmony inauguration event had finally settled. The mayor scheduled a charity gala next. Promoters lined up to secure slots in the rapidly filling event schedule.

Didi was on leave, sailing along the bays and fjords of the Stormy Sea as an able seaman on board a two-masted brig, which delivered basic supplies and mail to remote settlements along the coast. One night, off-watch and swinging with the roll of the sea in the hammock slung between forecastle beams, Didi checked mail. A message from Eka caught the eye.

> Hello everyone,
>
> A quick update on the quarterly evaluation of HAHAP benefits. In the first three months of operations, we've hosted two artistic/cultural events, including the blockbuster Save the Planet Awards ceremony, and three local business events. Also, the name 'Halls of Harmony' has become a permanent fixture in all kinds of media, which is great for our image and exposure.

> Overall, most critics have come to the conclusion that the Halls of Harmony is a great contribution to the promotion of art and culture in Artopolis. The mayor has been particularly generous in offering praise to Artophyle, awarding the City Hall Distinguished Service medals to Anan and myself.
>
> And last but not least, some of our new prospects seem to be considering doing business with us because of HAHAP's undivided success.
>
> Regards,
>
> Eka

So, Eka took care of the post-project management, the final cycle in the P3.express approach. Management activities in this group periodically reviewed benefit realisation and accrual one to five years after project closure. Typically, the project sponsor assumed this responsibility. It could eventually be the customer but never the project manager.

The sponsor could delegate the responsibility for benefit reviews to lower management roles, but not the accountability for the overall execution of post-project management cycle, starting with benefits evaluation.

This included both expected benefits listed in the project's benefits management plan and additional benefits, potential benefits and dis-benefits, too.

Benefits evaluation served as a reminder that projects aimed to realise benefits for the organisation, rather than simply produce the project product.

Benefit definition served as the key to benefit realisation. A vague, wordy description of the benefits served little purpose. Benefits could be tangible or intangible - reputation, image, exposure, market share or knowledge gains but needed to remain measurable against the baseline established in accordance with the benefits management plan.

G02 - Generate new ideas

AS A FOLLOW-ON to benefit reviews, the sponsor's responsibilities included generating ideas for additional benefit realisation. The result might be small, follow-on activities assigned to the operational teams, or possibly even suggestion of major add-ons that could be realised through new projects.

Didi fully agreed that the evaluation of benefits realised from completed projects presented a great source of ideas for future ones, particularly when benefit reviews focused on project bundles, rather than individual projects.

In the meantime, the brig had changed course and the roll of the hull changed to pitch. Didi didn't pay much attention, having developed sea legs two days after casting off. Hidden among the hog fuel and chippings of daily office operations, Didi discovered another – personal mail from Eka.

> Hi Didi,
> While I hope you are enjoying your time away from the office, there is a development that can't wait until your return.

> When reviewing the HAHAP benefits, I came up with the idea of convening a national conference on sustainable architecture, to be held in the Halls of Harmony (where else?).
>
> I thought of appointing Mirai as the project manager. Is it a good idea in your opinion?
>
> Regards,
>
> Eka

Didi struggled to stay awake amid the swinging of the hammock, but made an effort to fight off the sleep.

> Hello Eka,
>
> The conference you mention seems like a promising idea, but it requires assessment from the angle for the company's project portfolio, which is well above my level of competence.
>
> On your other point, I'm absolutely convinced that Mirai has a bright future in project management. While still a bit impulsive and prone to cutting corners, I believe Mirai would nonetheless make a good candidate for managing this project.
>
> While working on HAHAP, I never hesitated to ask Mirai to arrange all our workshops and meetings and they were always conducted perfectly. Mirai is a highly competent scheduler with an impressive academic background, already rounded off with some real-life experience. And last but not least, Mirai is a fountain of ideas and unorthodox approaches.
>
> The project you have in mind doesn't look to me too complicated, and I don't see why Mirai can't handle it.
>
> Kind regards,
>
> Didi

G03 - Conduct a focused communication

THE EARLIER MESSAGE Eka had circulated to project stakeholders fulfilled this final requirement of the post-project management activities group.

* * *

Satisfied with the results of the day's effort, Didi considered finally logging off and going to sleep, when the arrival of a new message raised a flag on the screen. It came from Anan, making Didi feel a tickling touch of intrigue. It's not every day that a CEO of a large and highly prominent company writes to the ranks. And Anan fully lived up to Didi's high expectations.

> Didi,
>
> I'm going down to Sanriol next month to check out some proposals sent to us by the new government. The military junta staged elections and gave the power back to a bunch of

civilians. Quite a few of Rilke's old cronies are back in the saddle. The Global Development Bank is also coming back and hurriedly looking for investment opportunities to catch up on the lost time.

The resounding success of HAHAP has firmly put Artophyle on the map and made it an attractive counterpart for big-league ventures.

I am fully aware of the highly competent support you provided to the late Rilke in advancing Artophyle's business interests in the region. I am equally aware of your insider knowledge of local below-the-radar opportunities for horse tourism. You may recall that I'm an avid hippophile.

On the strength of the above arguments, you'll be joining me on my visit. My office is making the necessary arrangements.

Regards,

Anan

PS. Forgot to mention that your contact Mo has made a stellar career becoming an important asset to Artophyle's objectives.

The pitching as good as subsided. A susurrant melody of the sea outside had replaced the thud of waves against the ancient wood of the hull. The fo'c'sle smelled of tar, hemp ropes and damp pijjakkers. Didi closed the eyes and dreamt of calm azure seas off Sanriol and the fragrance of coffee laced with cardamom.

The End